CW00327994

Dogs

This is a Parragon Book
This edition published in 2003

Parragon
Queen Street House
4 Queen Street
Bath BA1 1HE, UK

Copyright © Parragon 2002

ISBN: 1-40540-273-3

A copy of the CIP data for this book is available from the British Library upon request.

The right of Mary Waugh to be identified as the author of this work has been asserted in accordance with Section 77 of the Copyright, Designs and Patents Act of 1988.

Editorial, design and layout by Essential Books.

All pictures courtesy of Animals Unlimited.

Printed and bound in China

Dogs

Mary Waugh

Contents

Introduction

'Near this spot are deposited the remains of one who possessed beauty without vanity, strength without insolence, courage without ferocity, and all the virtues of Man without his vices.'
Lord Byron *Inscription on the Monument of a Newfoundland Dog,* 1808

The relationship between dog and man began over 15,000 years ago when our ancestors settled in camps and wolves scavenged the outskirts for food. These animals provided protection as they defended their food source from outsiders. It is thought that wolves effectively domesticated themselves, gradually transferring their bonding within an animal pack to a bond with humans, propelled by natural selection and environmental demands.

As time went on, humans realized how the instincts of wolves could be utilized to their advantage. They began to tame the more adaptable animals, almost certainly taking litters of cubs and training them. These wolves proved useful not only for guarding the encampment, guarding and herding sheep and cattle, but also for hunting down food. Gradually their duties expanded to include pulling loaded sledges and carts or hunting vermin. To improve the dogs' suitability for particular tasks, animals were selectively bred to enhance endurance, speed, stamina or size. Appearance was unimportant unless it affected an animal's ability to fulfil a certain function.

The earliest records of domesticated dogs date back to ancient Egyptian tomb paintings and Mesopotamian pottery, where we see dogs that closely resemble greyhounds being used for hunting. The Romans bred both this type and mastiff-type dogs – a large, powerful, short-haired breed used for hunting and in battle. Meanwhile in China, dogs were miniaturized and bred to be comforters and palace watchdogs. As trade routes opened up throughout the world, so different types of dog were introduced from country to country and used to create new breeds. In the Middle Ages, new varieties of hunting dog were bred to support the popular sport of hunting on horseback. Similarly, with the arrival of the shotgun, dogs were needed to find, flush out and retrieve game. Dogs were bred specifically for fighting and baiting sports, starting with the Roman mastiff and its descendants in

Introduction

gladiatorial contests, and continuing with bear and bull baiting, sports that continued into the nineteenth century. Smaller terriers were used in rat pits and for dog fights. Some dogs were bred for their speed and used for racing while others were bred for their agility in field trials. Because a dog's senses are more acute than those of a human, new work is constantly being found for them. During the twentieth century, for example, they have been trained to work with blind, deaf and disabled people. They also work with the police and the military.

The British and American Kennel Clubs were established in 1873 and 1884 respectively to establish breed standards for those breeds registered with them. The existence of these standards, together with the proliferation of competitive dog shows, has meant that greater emphasis has been placed on appearance over function. One of the consequences of this focus on appearance is inbreeding, which in turn has inevitably resulted in the emergence of genetic diseases peculiar to particular breeds.

The dog has a strong, resilient body that has adapted to fulfil the different demands that have been made of it. The same basic skeleton is present in all breeds.

A dog's body is primarily designed for running and endurance. Its senses are similar to those of a human but are more developed. It has a wider field of vision and is more sensitive to light and movement. Its ears are mobile and can catch sounds quickly and from a distance four times greater than that possible by a human. Its sense of touch lies mainly in the hairs around the muzzle and over the eyes, and in the paws. Although its sense of taste may be more limited than a human's, it has forty times more scent receptors, giving it a highly developed sense of smell.

With the exception of a few hairless varieties (and even they usually produce some hairy puppies in a litter), different breeds have very different coats. In fact, a dog's coat is often its defining feature. Dogs that evolved in warm climates have short, close coats while dogs in cold environments grew double coats (a water-resistant top coat and a warm, waterproof undercoat). Typically, a dog sheds its coat in the spring and autumn, when a new one is necessary to cope with the change in climate.

Selective breeding is responsible for the greatest modification in a dog's body – over time its ears have gone from being alert and erect like the ears of the spitz-type breeds to being almost any shape, from the droopy ears of the hound to the folded ears of the Airedale terrier.

It is only over the last century that the emphasis has fallen on the dog as a pet. This is a relationship from which both man and dog benefit. In exchange for food, warmth and contact a dog will provide friendship, protection and pleasure. For many people dogs provide an emotional outlet, not to mention the physical and therapeutic advantages of taking them out for a walk. It is not for nothing that the dog is known as man's best friend.

This book is intended as an introduction to eighty of the most popular breeds of dog recognized by both the American and British Kennel Clubs. They are divided into seven groups: the hound group; the gundog group; the terrier group; the working group; the pastoral group; the toy group; and the utility group. Each entry is designed to help you choose the best dog for your circumstances. It gives a brief description of the origins of the breed, its appearance, temperament and suitability as a pet. There is also a rating checklist for each breed, giving the average height, weight and lifespan of the dog plus grooming, feeding and exercise needs.

How to choose a dog

First decide which breed will best suit you. Whether you are single, have a family or are elderly or infirm, whether you live in the town or country, in a flat or large house with a garden should all influence your decision.

Learn about the breed you are interested in. How much exercise does it need? How much grooming is required? Can you afford the feeding, insurance and veterinary costs? Have you the space in your home for your new pet? Will everyone in your family get on with the breed you have in mind? Who will look after the dog if you are at work?

If buying a pedigree or pure-bred puppy, go to a reputable breeder. Consult the Kennel Club if in doubt. Older dogs have the advantage of being house-trained and should respond to basic commands.

Mongrels are unique, easy to train and less prone to inherited disease than pure-bred dogs. Go to a pet rescue centre or ask your vet or the Kennel Club for possible sources. Steer clear of pet shops unless you know they're reputable. You often can't check the parentage so you have no idea what you are buying.

Remember: a dog is for life.

What to look for

When choosing a puppy from a litter, look at the litter and watch how the puppies interact with one another. One may be bolder than the rest, bravely approaching you, while another may hang back beside its mother. Try to meet both parents so that you can get an idea of how your puppy is likely to look and behave when it gets older. Make sure you ask the breeder if he or she knows of any genetic problems.

A good puppy should have bright, alert eyes with no discharge. Its nose should be cool and damp. Its gums should be pink and its breath fresh. Its ears should be clean. Its coat should be shiny and clean with skin that has no parasites, spots or scabs. Its weight should be evenly distributed on all four legs and it should move fluently.

When choosing an adult dog, try to find out what you can about its background, from the owners or pet rescue centre. Watch how it reacts to other dogs and people and whether it responds to commands. You may want a vet to check its health before you commit yourself. It may have behavioural problems and so will need gentle handling, possibly with the aid of a pet behaviourist. Your vet will be able to advise you where to find one.

Essential equipment

All dogs need a collar, lead and name tag. The collar and lead can be leather, nylon or chain, depending on the weight and strength of the dog and the degree of control needed. Avoid chain collars for puppies and very small breeds. For a puppy, a training lead is a good investment to ensure you retain control while the puppy is still learning commands. If your dog is very powerful, a body harness may help with control. Even if your dog is microchipped, it is wise to give it an identity tag with your phone number on it. If it has a tendency to bite, you will need a muzzle.

All dogs need a bed, which should be comfortable and washable. Wicker baskets, plastic baskets and bean bags are available but dogs will be happy to have a box with a blanket inside. Indoor kennels keep the puppy out of harm's way, provide a safe place for it when you're out of the room and are a convenient way of house-training.

Food bowls and water bowls should be strong and kept hygienically clean. Whether long or shorthaired, all dogs will need a brush and a comb for grooming. Although toys are not strictly essential, they can be useful in providing something to chew on, to pull against or chase.

Feeding and nutrition

Your dog must be given a well-balanced diet. Although dogs love meat, they need a varied diet containing proteins, carbohydrates, vitamins, minerals, fats and water. Brand-name dog foods are either dry, canned or semi-moist. It is important to get the right balance and amount for the age, size and breed of your dog. Fresh vegetables are also recommended. Seek advice from your vet if you are unsure. Fresh clean water must be available at all times.

Puppies need up to five small meals a day until they are six months old. From then on, two meals are enough. This may be reduced to one when the dog reaches adulthood. Start them off on whatever the breeder has fed them and introduce new foods gradually.

Each dog should have its own dish and its own feeding place to ensure it is sufficiently nourished. After twenty minutes, even if the meal is unfinished, remove the bowls and wash them.

Rather than giving chocolate rewards, stick to nutritious dog treats or chews. Bones should be raw beef bones. Avoid cooked bones or others that may splinter or get stuck in the throat.

House-training

Dogs are clean animals and do not like dirtying their own territory, particularly their eating and sleeping places.

Choose a spot for your puppy's toilet. This should be outside or near the door to the outside. Take your puppy there when it wakes up, after it has drunk water, finished playing or fifteen minutes after every meal. Establish a routine, use a key phrase each time you go there, and gradually it will associate the word/s with the act of elimination. When it has performed successfully in the right place, heap praise on your pet.

Many people swear by using a indoor kennel as the puppy's private place, where it can sleep and play in safety. The puppy will not want to soil this private place so will quickly learn to wait until taken outside. Alternatively, spread newspaper near the door, reducing the area of paper day by day. Gradually, with your encouragement, the puppy will learn to wait until it can go outside.

There is no point shouting at your puppy, hitting it or rubbing its nose in the mess. It will not understand. Instead, watch it carefully and at the first sign distract it and immediately take it outside to the correct spot.

Grooming

All dogs need grooming of some sort. Hairless dogs need regular baths with a shampoo that will ward off skin problems. Short smooth coats need only a weekly rub with a rubber brush and cloth to reduce shedding and produce a gleaming coat. Other dogs need regular brushing to remove tangles, dirt and matting. Some dogs will need to be stripped (removing the old hair with a special brush and comb to thin it out) or clipped roughly every three months. The long coats of the smaller breeds are the highest maintenance and need frequent brushing and washing.

It is important to have the right grooming equipment. Take advice from your pet shop or vet if you are unsure.

Eyes and ears need to be regularly checked and cleaned. Feet should be cleaned regularly, the hair trimmed where necessary and the nails clipped carefully. Canine toothbrushes and toothpaste if used properly will help eliminate smelly breath and gum disease.

Dogs only need bathing once a month. Brush the coat thoroughly then wash with dog shampoo. Rub dry and leave the dog in a warm room to dry off completely. Long-haired or double-coated breeds may need blow-drying.

Training

Dogs aren't born well behaved. Good behaviour needs to be taught from an early age through good training. A dog that obeys its owner's commands is appreciated by everyone. If it will sit, lie down, stay, come and heel on command, it will cause few problems.

Your dog must understand what sort of behaviour is acceptable to you and what is not, both inside and outside your home. Training depends on routine and patience. Decide on the rules of your house and stick to them. Encourage good behaviour by reinforcing it with rewards – either praise or a treat. Physical punishment and shouting are always counterproductive.

One person in your home should have prime responsibility for training the dog. This should be the person who spends most time with it. Other members of the family should follow the trainer's example.

Training sessions should be kept short but frequent. A dog learns through repetition and consistency. It is a good idea to begin training it somewhere quiet without distractions. Eventually, as your dog becomes more reliable, you will be able to move to more public places.

Introduction

Obedience classes are a good idea for the inexperienced owner and the problem dog. Not only do they help train the dog but, perhaps more importantly, they train the owner in training and ownership skills.

Key to rating checklist

Exercise:		
	***	two 30-minute runs a day
	**	two 20-minute runs a day
	*	one 10-20 minute walk a day
Grooming	***	15 minutes brushing a day
	**	5-10 minutes brushing a day
	*	2-3 minutes brushing a day

The checklist is not the gospel; it is a rough guide. Every dog is different. Exercise needs in particular depend on a dog's character. Use the ratings as a benchmark but modify them if necessary once you get to know your dog well.

The hound group

The hound group is one of the oldest groups of dog, originating thousands of years ago when man discovered the breed's skill at cornering, catching and killing prey. A wide variety of breeds exists within the group, which divides into two types: scent hounds and sight hounds.

Sight hounds originate in southwest Asia, with breeds such as the Saluki, Afghan and Borzoi, which were seen as hounds of the nobility and were associated with royal houses. It is believed that hounds were introduced to Europe by Phoenician traders more than 2,500 years ago. In Great Britain, they were cross-bred with mastiff breeds to produce sturdier, more resilient dogs such as the Scottish deerhound or Irish wolfhound. The English Greyhound and the Whippet are elegant, streamlined creatures with bodies designed to move after their prey at great speed. Though still used for hunting in the Middle East, they are more commonly used as show or domestic animals. Their love of running and their independent nature mean they do not always respond easily to training as a pet. They need daily access to wide open spaces where they can exercise safely. They are generally calm in temperament though they do not make ideal companions for children.

Scent hounds have a more recent history than sight hounds. These were bred to track by using their nose rather than their eyes. They first came into their own in medieval France when numerous varieties were developed, particularly the griffon and the basset types. The St Hubert hound originated in a sixth-century Ardennes monastery and was delivered annually to the French king by successive generations of monks. It was eventually introduced to England by William the Conqueror, the bloodhound being one of its closest descendants.

Among the smaller scent hounds are the harriers, which are similar in looks to foxhounds and were first established in Britain in the thirteenth century. Unlike sight hounds, which remain silent at work, scent hounds will bark or howl when they find a scent. Characteristics of the breed include pendulous ears and lips that aid their tracking skills, sturdy legs that enable prolonged work and a tenacious appetite for tracking. Intelligent, tolerant and friendly, they can make good pets but have an independent streak that can be difficult to control.

Afghan Hound

This regal breed has an air of sophistication all of its own. Lean, swift and elegant, it is still used for hunting and as a guard dog in Afghanistan, where its coat protects it from the extreme winter cold. It has become a popular show dog and pet for those with commitment.

Origins Its history can be traced back to the Middle East. Used to hunt gazelle, deer and leopard, it is fleet of foot and extremely agile in rough terrain. Also used as a guard dog for sheep and cattle, it was introduced to Britain and America in the 1920s.

Appearance Three varieties exist in Afghanistan, short-haired, fringe-haired and long-haired. Its coat can be any colour. It has ears that are long and set back, and dark eyes in a long, elegant face. Its legs are long and straight and it has unusually large feet for a sight hound.

Temperament Loving and affectionate, though occasionally aloof, the Afghan also makes a good watchdog. It is an energetic animal that needs regular exercise and thorough obedience training to curb its independent streak.

Suitability as a pet High maintenance in terms of grooming, which should be done daily. The Afghan is not aggressive and gets on with children but may become frustrated without sufficient exercise.

Right The Afghan is noted for its paws which are larger than those of other similar-sized breeds

Above The Afghan has an aloof character which is expressed in the noble carriage of its head and the almost defiant look in its eyes

Height 64–74 cm (25–9 in)
Weight 23–7 kg (50–60 lb)
Life span 12–14 years
Grooming ✳✳✳
Exercise ✳✳✳
Town or Country T/C

Basenji

The most notable characteristic of this sight hound is that it does not bark but makes a yodelling sound when happy. It is a fastidious dog that will clean itself rather like a cat. The female is unusual in that she only comes into season once a year.

Origins It is possible that the Basenji originated in the Middle East, its likeness having been depicted on Egyptian tombs. The dog we know today, however, came from Africa where it was used for hunting. It was introduced to Britain and America in the 1930s.

Appearance A short-coated dog with sharp upstanding ears and a tightly curled tail. Its wrinkled brow gives it an endearingly concerned appearance. Its sleek, short-haired coat comes in black, black and white, tan and white or brindle (brown or grey streaks or patches against a darker colour).

Temperament Good-natured and companionable. It can be mischievous and likes to climb. It has a reputation for stealing food and is not always responsive to training.

The hound group

Suitability as a pet Like many hounds, it can be difficult to train so needs regular handling from an early age. It is naturally curious and loves to play. A gentle, affectionate dog that will suit many households.

Right Constantly alert, the Basenji always looks ready for action

Above The Basenji makes a particularly effective hunter because it goes after its prey in silence

Height 41–3 cm (16–17 in)
Weight 9.5–11 kg (21–4 lb)
Life span 12 years
Grooming *
Exercise * *
Town or Country T/C

Basset Hound

Best known as the cartoon character Fred Basset, this scent hound (sometimes known as a Hush Puppy) has also been associated with comfortable shoes all round the world. Its distinctive appearance and deep foghorn voice make it stand out in a crowd.

Origins A descendant of the French Bassets ('bas' meaning low), the basset hound is a distant relative of the bloodhound and was bred to chase hares. It may be slow but it can steadily cover considerable distances.

Appearance The Basset Hound has a barrel-like body atop short, sturdy legs. It seems to have more skin than strictly necessary, which wrinkles over its body. Its ears are long, possibly to aid in picking up scent, while its gentle eyes are slightly sunken in its distinctive dome-shaped head. Its coat is short, smooth and comes in combinations of black, tan, white and lemon.

Temperament A gentle, kindly dog that is good with children. Its one negative characteristic is its occasional stubbornness. It has a hearty appetite that must be watched if it is not to put on weight.

The hound group

Suitability as a pet A dog with a great character that can adapt well to life in the city. Its appealing, friendly temperament should make it a good family member. Its enormous bark makes a great burglar deterrent.

Right The Basset Hound's long ears and drooping eyes give it a melancholic look that belies its true character

Left Its gait is lumbering but the Basset Hound can reliably cover long distances

Height 33–38 cm (13–15 in)
Weight 18–27 kg (40–60 lb)
Life span 12 years
Grooming *
Exercise *
Town or Country T/C

Beagle

An eager hunter, the Beagle can also make a lively and affectionate family dog, provided there is plenty of space where it can exercise. It loves human companionship and being part of a group although it can be obstinate when being trained.

Origins The Beagle has existed since the fourteenth century, when it was bred for hunting rabbits. It can vary in size and appearance between countries – in Britain the smallest beagles once accompanied mounted hunters, fitting snugly in their saddlebags. A working dog until the 1940s, when it became domesticated.

Appearance Its smooth or wiry short-haired coat comes in any hound colour and is conveniently waterproof. It has an appealing face with a slightly domed head and fine floppy ears. Its compact muscular body is designed for the speed of the chase. Its tail is white-tipped. It grows to 13–16 inches.

Temperament Friendly and playful but strong-willed and often difficult to train. If kept indoors for too long it may become bored and destructive.

The hound group

Suitability as a pet An engaging, friendly creature, the beagle is a pack animal that will fit well into family life in the country. It needs plenty of exercise to keep it happy. Care must be taken to instil the recall command because once it has a scent it is hard to distract.

Right Beagles love being a part of family life

Above The Beagle's well-defined muzzle is designed for closely following the scent of its prey

Height 33–40 cm (13–16 in)
Weight 8–14 kg (18–30 lb)
Life span 13 years
Grooming *
Exercise * * *
Town or Country C

Borzoi

A dignified, good-looking dog and superb hunter, this sight hound has become increasingly popular as a companion, although it is not recommended as a family dog.

Origins The Borzoi comes from the steppes of Russia, where it was worked in pairs by the Russian aristocracy to hunt wolves. It is thought to be the result of crossing a Greyhound with a Russian Sheepdog, to create a breed with the protective coat needed for the harsh Russian winters.

Appearance Tall, sleek and elegant, it has a long silky coat that varies in length over its body. The coat is usually white with various colours of markings. Its powerful head and neck are designed to grab its prey by the neck and wrestle it to the ground.

Temperament Though docile and self-contained, the borzoi can be jumpy around children. It needs considerable attention although it is not known for always giving affection in return. Its reactions are swift, and it is capable of becoming dangerous if annoyed beyond the limits of its patience.

The hound group

Suitability as a pet Although it can adapt to urban life, it needs space to run off the lead and will be happiest in a large house. It prefers to be left alone and unruffled. It will shed hair and should be groomed regularly.

Below The Borzoi has long, lean jaws that are powerful enough to seize its prey by the neck and hold it to the ground

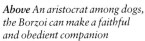

Above An aristocrat among dogs, the Borzoi can make a faithful and obedient companion

Height 69–79 cm (27–31 in)
Weight 35–48 kg (75–105 lb)
Life span 11–13 years
Grooming * * *
Exercise * * *
Town or Country C

Dachshund

Known widely as the 'Sausage Dog', this scent hound must be one of the most recognizable breeds in the world. In fact, its name means 'badger dog', and reflects its original use as a working hunter. Today the Dachshund is a popular household pet.

Origins Dogs resembling the smooth-haired Dachshund appear on ancient Egyptian sculptures. More recently they were bred in Germany as hunting dogs whose courageousness and size made them ideal for following badgers, weasels and foxes to earth.

Appearance The Dachshund comes in two sizes, miniature (under 5 inches) and standard (5–10 inches). Its body is twice as long as it is high, with short legs and a strong chest. It holds its head boldly and has an alert, intelligent expression. Its coat comes in three types: smooth-haired, wire-haired and long-haired.

Temperament A quiet, obedient and affectionate dog that can be difficult to house-train. Dachshunds make great companions and guard dogs, with a big bark that will unnerve any intruder.

The hound group

Suitability as a pet The standard-size Dachshund is an ideal family pet. It is robust, has lots of character and needs little exercise or grooming (though the long-haired variety requires more attention). Miniature Dachshunds are more fragile and less suited to family life.

A small dog with a huge personality that has won the hearts of many owners for its companionship and undemanding nature

Height (standard) 13–25 cm (5–10 in)
Weight (standard) 6.5–11.5 kg (15–25 lb)
Life span 14–17 years
Grooming *
Exercise *
Town or Country T/C

Greyhound

One of the oldest known sight hounds, noted for its great speed and hunting prowess. Despite its reputation in the field and on the track, it can be a surprisingly docile and relaxed companion.

Origins Greyhounds were favoured by the Egyptians, who frequently mummified them and buried them with their owners. They were brought to the UK in the fifth century, when they were used as a hunting dog. The sport of Greyhound racing began in the fifteenth century, though it wasn't introduced to America until the 1920s.

Appearance Lean, muscular and beautifully proportioned, the greyhound is capable of achieving speeds of up to 45 mph. Its long, straight legs support a sleek body with a deep chest and flat-skulled head. Its coat is short and comes in a variety of colours.

Temperament Greyhounds have a finely developed chase instinct and, unless carefully trained, will set off after almost anything that moves. They are gentle, sensitive dogs but can become neurotic if confined in small spaces without the opportunity to run.

The hound group

Suitability as a pet Retired racing Greyhounds make good family pets but beware of letting them off the lead in a park where there are smaller breeds or squirrels to chase. They are good with children but need socializing from an early age to become the ideal companion.

Despite appearances, greyhounds need little exercise and are known as the 'couch potato' of the dog world

Height 69–76 cm (27–30 in)
Weight 27–32 kg (60–70 lb)
Life span 10–12 years
Grooming *
Exercise * * *
Town or Country T/C

Irish Wolfhound

Despite its hunting history, the Irish Wolfhound is one of the sweetest-natured dogs around. Once believed to have magical and human powers, these sight hounds were extremely successful hunters.

Origins The Irish Wolfhound was valued by the Irish chieftains for its skill in hunting wolf, deer and elk, as well as in defending its masters. So successful was it at its job that the need for it as good as disappeared and the breed began to die out until a British Army officer, Captain G. A. Graham, helped re-establish it.

Appearance The biggest dog of all, its rough, wiry coat comes in a variety of colours. It has a muscular, well-proportioned body with a proud, long head that has a slight indentation between the eyes. Its legs are long, straight and strong.

Temperament The Irish Wolfhound is a gentle giant. It is a loyal and kind dog that can adapt to most living conditions, provided it gets reasonable exercise. Its size is off-putting enough to most strangers. This, coupled with its loud bark, makes it a great guard dog.

The hound group

Suitability as a pet One of the least aggressive dogs, the Irish wolfhound can make a wonderful family pet, provided there is the space to accommodate it. It will be patient with children and become their dependable and affectionate companion.

Right A gentle, dignified dog which can achieve great speeds when allowed to run free

Above The Irish Wolfhound has a rough wiry coat which grows longer round the eyes and jaw

Height 71–90 cm (28–35 in)
Weight 40–55 kg (90–120 lb)
Life span 11 years
Grooming *
Exercise * * *
Town or Country C

Rhodesian Ridgeback

Named because of the curious ridge of hair that grows along its spine against the direction of the rest of the coat, the Rhodesian Ridgeback is a powerful but dignified scent hound.

Origins Its predecessors are known to have existed as guard dogs and hunters in southern Africa. When European settlers arrived, they bred their own mastiffs and scent hounds with the native dogs to produce the dogs we know today. Ridgebacks guarded property and were used to track lions.

Appearance A muscular dog that is extremely strong. It has a short, sleek coat that ranges from red to wheaten (pale yellow). Its muzzle can be dark and there may be a flash of white on its chest. When attentive, its brow wrinkles gently in concentration.

Temperament Surprisingly mild, given its appearance. This is a dog that will stick loyally to its master and deter any intruders. It can be reserved with strangers. It is brave, intelligent and faithful, although not always reliable with other dogs.

Suitability as a pet Not ideal for first-time owners or families with young children. These dogs need to be trained well before they get too big to manage. They have immense stamina and need considerable exercise.

Right The combination of its solid frame and height make the Ridgeback a large powerful dog which will deter any intruder

Above A strong physique can be coupled with an almost hypnotic gaze

Height 61–9 cm (24–7 in)
Weight 30–9 kg (65–85 lb)
Life span 12 years
Exercise * * *
Grooming *
Town or Country T/C

Saluki

Also known as the 'Gazelle Hound', the Saluki has great agility and endurance, which used to enable it to hunt gazelle over rough terrain. Hawks were trained to slow the prey down until the Saluki held it, awaiting the kill.

Origins Originating in the Middle East, the Saluki was the much-prized hunting companion of the Bedouin. It was considered the gift of Allah and could only be given from one person to another, never sold. According to fundamentalist Islam, all dogs were unclean except for the Saluki, which was admitted into its owner's tent.

Appearance Built for speed, this sight hound can achieve up to 40 mph. It has a deep chest and long, straight legs. Its graceful head tapers towards the nose and has small, deep-set, far-seeing eyes. Its coat may be smooth or feathered and comes in a variety of colours.

Temperament Loyal but independent, the Saluki can be aloof when it meets strangers. It is an active breed that likes the outdoors and needs long daily walks. It is a sensitive animal that may respond badly to rough handling and noise.

Suitability as a pet Its highly-strung nature does not make it an ideal family pet. However, it does make a faithful companion to those prepared to provide it with the regular exercise and grooming it requires.

Right The legs of the Saluki are long and strong, with powerful thigh muscles which makes them fast on the ground and able to leap over obstacles

Above A Saluki pup. The elegant head has gentle, far-seeing eyes and softly-feathered ears

Height 58–71 cm (23–8 in)
Weight 14–25 kg (31–55 lb)
Life span 12 years
Grooming * *
Exercise * * *
Town or Country T/C

Whippet

An adaptable small relation of the Greyhound, this sight hound is still used for coursing and racing, as well as for companionship. Its love of home comforts contrasts with its determined and fearless nature in the field.

Origins In nineteenth-century northern England, coursing terriers were crossed with Greyhounds to produce the Whippet, a dog with the speed necessary for catching rabbits.

Appearance Its lean, fragile appearance belies a body of great stamina, capable of reaching speeds of 40 mph. Its coat is short and fine-haired and can be in blocks of a range of colours, brindled or patchy. Its broad tapering head has alert, brown eyes. Its tail curls between its hind legs when it is still.

Temperament A gentle and friendly animal that will stick by its owner through thick and thin. Its coursing instincts may well need to be curbed by firm obedience training, to which the whippet will respond well, but it is a dog that loves the outdoors and the opportunity to run free.

Suitability as a pet The Whippet makes an obedient and affectionate pet but may become nervous if it is around rowdy or young children. Be prepared for lots of exercise if it is not to become neurotic.

Below The long lean tail is carried between the legs when the dog is still

Above The Whippet is the smallest of the sight hounds

Height 47–51 cm (18.5–20 in)
Weight 12.5–13.5 kg (27–30 lb)
Life span 13–14 years
Grooming *
Exercise * * *
Town or Country T/C

The gundog (sporting) group

Dogs have accompanied man on hunting expeditions for thousands of years. It was not until the eighteenth and nineteenth centuries when the development of firearms led to an expansion of the breeds trained to work with a huntsman with a gun, that gundogs became established. Unlike many of their predecessors, gundogs do not capture the quarry but may flush, track, point or retrieve it. They contribute with their enhanced senses of hearing and smell. These dogs are usually hard-working, energetic and obedient. Their generous, co-operative nature tends to make them excellent companions and family dogs.

When choosing a gundog, the nature of the terrain and the quarry are the two principal considerations. Gundogs generally fall into five categories: spaniels ('flushing dogs') that work in scrubland; setters and pointers that work in open moorland; retrievers that fetch the game; water dogs that retrieve from lakes and ponds; and HPR (hunt, point and retrieve) breeds that perform all three duties.

Spaniels are represented on Roman ceramics, on the Bayeux Tapestry and are mentioned for the first time in

Chaucer's *Canterbury Tales*. They are thought to have originated in Spain and been brought to Britain by the Romans. Originally used to flush out game for the huntsmen's nets, falcons or hounds, they became the natural companion of armed hunters.

Setters and pointers are probably derived from the Spanish pointing hound, imported to Europe and America during the sixteenth century. Pointers follow the scent of their prey and then stand stock still with one foreleg raised and nose pointing the way, allowing the hunters to go forward. Setters perform the same role, except that they lower themselves close to the ground or 'set' when they see the game and then flush it out.

Retrievers have an innate gentleness that allows them to retrieve prey in their mouth without harming it. They respond well to training and are known for their work as service dogs as well as in the field. Water dogs, which include the Irish Water Spaniel, Chesapeake Bay Retriever and Curly-coated Retriever, have a natural love of swimming. The HPR breeds come mostly from the European mainland. They include the German Pointers, Hungarian Vizla, Italian Spinone and the Weimaraner.

American Cocker Spaniel

Smaller than its English counterpart, the American Cocker Spaniel is often calmer and more obedient too. They are both renowned for their lively and affectionate personality.

Origins The English Cocker Spaniel was introduced into America, some say by the pilgrims aboard the *Mayflower*, as a hunter of small birds. American breeders worked to obtain a different dog during the 1930s and 1940s until the American Cocker Spaniel was recognized by the American Kennel Club in 1946.

Appearance This breed has a short muzzle and a round dome of a head. It has a higher shoulder and a shorter, more sloping back than its English counterpart. Its coat is fine and silky, being left long on the ears, legs and abdomen. The coat comes in a wide range of colour combinations.

Temperament A lively, energetic and playful dog that is generally a friendly and responsive companion. Unscrupulous breeding practices have meant that it can be an unpredictable animal so take care to check the breeder's credentials when buying.

Suitability as a pet It will fit happily into a family but needs a considerable amount of exercise and grooming. It does not like being restricted to confined spaces though it is easily trained and obedient once it gets outside.

Above A playful, fun-loving dog which has become a popular pet in America. Its fine, thick hair needs regular grooming

Height 35–8 cm (14–15 in)
Weight 11–13 kg (24–8 lb)
Life span 13–14 years
Grooming ***
Exercise ***
Town or Country T/C

Clumber Spaniel

The clumber spaniel looks unlike any other spaniel. It is heavier, slower and has a more stand-offish attitude.

Origins Its origins are untraceable. It is believed that, in 1768, the French Duc de Nouailles presented some spaniels to the Second Duke of Newcastle, who then established a kennel at his estate in Clumber Park. Others suggest it was developed by crossing the Alpine spaniel and the basset or even the St Bernard.

Appearance It has a long back and short, sturdy legs suitable for a steady day's hunting. Its skin is loose, particularly on its forehead and its eyelids droop. Its coat is fine and easily groomed and is often white with occasional orange or lemon markings.

Temperament A kindly creature that used to be part of a team of dogs that worked methodically together to beat the game towards the hunters.

Suitability as a pet A very biddable animal, it can make a good family pet although the breed has lost its popularity over the years. Its intelligent, gentle nature makes it a loyal and loving companion.

The gundog group

Right The Clumber Spaniel is a less active dog than its relations

Left It has become a rare breed but makes a good, undemanding pet althought its old hunting instincts may easily surface

Height 48–51 cm (19–20 in)
Weight 29–36 kg (65–80 lb)
Life span 12–13 years
Grooming **
Exercise **
Town or Country T/C

English Cocker Spaniel

A delightful small dog that is still used as a hunting dog but also makes one of the most popular and attractive canine additions to the family.

Origins Thought to have originated in Spain before the fifteenth century, spaniels were used as hunting dogs to flush out game ('starters') and retrieve the quarry, usually woodcock ('cockers'). They were developed in Wales and southwest England.

Appearance It has a well-defined head, less domed than its American relative, with a long nose for scenting. Its ears are long and tend to get in the way of eating and drinking. Its coat is fine and silky, and needs regular grooming and brushing. It comes in black, liver, red, gold or white, with markings or ticking in black, liver or red.

Temperament Incredibly eager to please, the Cocker Spaniel is a tremendously enthusiastic small dog whose whole hindquarters wag when it is pleased. It has a strong personality, retaining its independence while joining in family life to the full.

Suitability as a pet The Cocker Spaniel can be excitable and so needs regular exercise. It is affectionate and will enthusiastically join in with children's games. Its nose is always to the ground following a scent, an instinct that can get it lost if it is not watched.

The Cocker Spaniel is a popular family pet which need plenty of exercise and regular grooming

Height 38–41 cm (15–16 in)
Weight 13–15 kg (28–32 lb)
Life span 13–14 years
Grooming * *
Exercise * * *
Town or Country T/C

English Pointer

The English Pointer is a handsome, even-tempered animal, bred for accompanying the shoot. Having sighted the prey, it would stand and point while the Greyhounds hunted it down. Used less in Britain as a hunting dog today than in America.

Origins The pointer's distinguished features have graced English art and writing since the seventeenth century. It is a breed that was developed in England in response to the need for a talented hunting dog. It is widely thought to be the result of a cross between the Spanish Pointer and Fox- or Bloodhound for scenting, the Greyhound for speed and the Bull Terrier for general pluck.

Appearance An elegant, well-proportioned dog which has a distinctive dish-shaped head, its skull as long as its muzzle. Its fine hard coat can be lemon, orange, black or liver with white.

Temperament An obedient, hard-working dog which has bags of energy and brio. It has a sensitive nature that is both biddable and generous.

Suitability as a pet An adaptable dog that suits family life as well as life in the field. Its benign nature makes it good with children. Needs lots of exercise so needs access to plenty of wide open space.

Below The dog's noble head is of a shape such that the nose can be raised for scenting

Above The English Pointer stands immobile, pointing the direction of its prey

Height 61–9 cm (24–7 in)
Weight 20–30 kg (44–66 lb)
Life span 12–13 years
Grooming *
Exercise * * *
Town or Country T/C

English Setter

A reliable, good-natured and considerate dog. Its proud carriage and distinctive coat make it a particularly handsome breed.

Origins It is thought that the setter developed as a result of crossing other hunting breeds, particularly spaniels and pointers. Originally used as a bird hunter in the sixteenth century, it was in 1825 that an Englishman, Edward Lavarack, and a Welshman, R. L. Purcell Llewellin, perfected the breed, improving its scenting ability and speed.

Appearance A handsome dog with a long, rectangular head. It has a flat coat with feathering on the ears, chest, abdomen, undersides of the thighs, backs of the legs and tail. It is white with markings in a pattern known as Belton (after an English village). These may be brown, black, liver or tan and are flecked through the coat.

Temperament Sociable and intelligent, the English Setter loves exercise. It is very responsive to training and makes an efficient gundog, searching out pheasant, grouse or partridge, stopping and setting on to them.

Suitability as a pet Although it can be high-spirited, the Setter is a marvellous family dog, provided it gets enough exercise. It is affectionate, good with children and has plenty of energy. Regular grooming will keep its coat in good condition.

A first-rate hunting dog, the English Setter. Its distinctive markings, soft eyes and gentle, though occasionally exuberant, nature make it a handsome and energetic companion

Height 61–9 cm (24–7 in)
Weight 25–30 kg (55–66 lb)
Life span 12–13 years
Grooming * *
Exercise * * *
Town or Country C

English Springer Spaniel

With an active, high-spirited and devoted personality, the springer spaniel makes a bouncy household pet and remains a tireless worker in the field.

Origins It is thought that the Romans may have introduced the spaniel to Britain from Spain. Similar dogs to the English Springer appear in drawings and prints of the sixteenth and seventeenth centuries. They were the larger dogs in a litter and used to 'spring' or flush the game from thickets. The first Springer was imported from England to Canada in 1913.

Appearance The breed has diverged into two types: field and show spaniels. The field dog is active, with a lean face and hunting instincts; the show dog is heavier with long fur and ears, and little instinct for the chase. Springers are a little taller than other spaniels with a close, straight coat of either liver or chocolate and white.

Temperament This dog loves constant activity and has apparently limitless energy. It loves company and thrives on physical and mental stimulation. It is easily trained to play games and can make a good watchdog.

Suitability as a pet Springers tend to be happy, uncomplicated dogs that are affectionate, content and good with children and other dogs. They can be too boisterous for some households as they need considerable attention if they are not to become bored.

A dog that loves the opportunity to play a game. Its boundless energy makes it a demanding companion

Height 48–51 cm (19–20 in)
Weight 22–4 kg (49–52 lb)
Life span 12–14 years
Grooming * *
Exercise * *
Town or Country T/C

German Pointer

An energetic, versatile dog bred specifically for its hunting abilities, the pointer searches by scenting out its prey, then 'pointing' the way for the hunter with its nose.

Origins The original German Pointers were much heavier dogs than those of today. In the nineteenth century, they were crossed with the English Pointer to give a more alert and athletic version. Cross-breeding with Irish and Gordon Setters gave the long-haired version while a cross with the Pudelpointer and French Griffon produced the hardy, versatile Wire-haired Pointer.

Appearance Designed for hunting, the Pointer has a lean, muscular body with a keen nose and great stamina. Its coat can be smooth and shiny, in combinations of black and white or black, white and liver. The Wire-haired variety is thicker set and has a rough coat that keeps it warm while working in cold or water.

Temperament A real all-round dog that enjoys a busy working life but can make a loving pet. It is faithful, good-natured and tolerant of children. The Wire-haired variety can be aggressive towards other dogs when riled.

Suitability as a pet This is a dog that needs lots of exercise if it's not working. It is not best-suited to life in the town unless there is a lot of space for it to run about. It is strong-willed and can be difficult to train unless the owner is experienced and firm.

The short-haired German Pointer is an athletic dog of elegant proportions and an alert, far-seeing expression

Height 60–5 cm (24–6 in)
Weight 27–32 kg (60–70 lb)
Life span 12–14 years
Grooming *
Exercise * * *
Town or Country C

Golden Retriever

The Golden Retriever is one of the most popular family dogs. Relaxed, responsive, affectionate and loyal – what more could you want?

Origins At the end of the nineteenth century Lord Tweedmouth developed this breed for retrieving shot waterfowl on his estate near Inverness in Scotland. Golden Retrievers were first exhibited in competitions in England in the early 1900s. Although they made their way to America with travellers before the 1900s, they were not exhibited there for some years, in fact until after 1920.

Appearance A strong, muscular dog with a dense, water-repellant coat that can be straight or wavy. The legs and tail are feathered while the coat colour can vary from pale cream to golden. The eyes are alert, gentle and intelligent.

Temperament A self-confident dog with a kind, gentle, intelligent manner. It is trustworthy, reliable and affectionate, needing a long daily walk with the chance to run free and even to swim.

Suitability as a pet Although patient with children and loyal, the Retriever does need careful training to channel its energy and friendliness. Its coat sheds a lot of hair, so it's not for the house-proud.

One of the most popular domestic dogs, the Golden Retriever is also known for its reliability as a guide dog and its effectiveness when working as a sniffer dog with the police

Height 51–61 cm (20–4 in)
Weight 27–36 kg (60–80 lb)
Life span 12–13 years
Grooming * *
Exercise * * *
Town or Country T/C

Gordon Setter

More solidly built than the other setters, this is the heavyweight of the breed. Less stylish than its English or Irish relations but a sound working dog with plenty of stamina.

Origins Originally known as the black and tan setter in the seventeenth century, the breed was then standardized by the fourth Duke of Richmond and Gordon. He bred the dogs for game shooting on the Scottish moors, where their qualities of strength and endurance were called into play.

Appearance Always has a long, silky black and tan coat that is feathered on its ears, chest, legs, abdomen and tail. The rich tan markings are particularly defined on its muzzle and legs, with a spot over each eye.

Temperament Calmer than its Irish and English counterparts, the Gordon Setter has a very pleasant, extrovert personality but holds itself with reserve when it meets strangers. It is relaxed, loyal and obedient but has boundless energy and can be a bit much in a confined space.

Suitability as a pet It gets on with children and other dogs but needs a great deal of exercise to work off its energy. Loving, affectionate but occasionally over-enthusiastic.

Below The Gordon Setter is a reliable working dog with all the strength and stamina required for a long day in the field

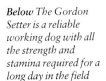

Above Heavier built than the other setters, it is more powerful but slower too

Height 62–6 cm (24–6 in)
Weight 25–30 kg (56–66 lb)
Life span 12–13 years
Grooming * *
Exercise * * *
Town or Country C

Irish Setter

Much admired for its gleaming chestnut coat, this is definitely the most high-spirited of the setters. It has bags of energy to burn and is unlikely to thrive in an urban environment.

Origins The Irish setter's ascendants are thought to include the old Spanish Pointer and early Scottish Setters. Like its setter relations, it was bred to find game birds then remain absolutely still while its master shot and netted them.

Appearance Not a heavy dog but one that is well muscled so that it can perform well on the hunting field. Its coat is luxuriantly feathered and always shiny, sometimes with a flash of white on its brisket. Its distinctive almond-shaped eyes are always kind and gentle.

Temperament Exuberant and outgoing, the Irish setter is known for its high-octane energy and general *joie de vivre*. Its enthusiasm on meeting strangers is unbounded and it can be relied on not to know when to calm down.

The gundog group

Suitability as a pet A more high-maintenance pet could not be found. Training can be time-consuming and regular grooming is essential. Easily distracted, playful and affectionate, this is a dog that needs a lot of exercise.

The Red Setter thrives on activity and is known for its wild but effusively friendly nature. This is a dog that needs a firm hand to curb its boisterousness and make it come when called

Height 58–69 cm (25–7 in)
Weight 27–32 kg (60–70 lb)
Life span 12–13 years
Grooming * *
Exercise * * *
Town or Country C

Irish Water Spaniel

The largest spaniel of the lot, this is a dog that is primarily a retriever. Energetic, intelligent and affectionate, it is a first-rate gundog although too boisterous to have made a popular house dog.

Origins It was developed in Ireland from two strains in the north and south of the country. It is thought that it may have been developed from the Portuguese Water Dog, which was brought over from Portugal to Ireland by fishermen, or from the poodle. In the nineteenth century a Dubliner, Justin McCarthy, fixed the breed type.

Appearance Its distinctive coat makes the Irish Water Spaniel stand out from the other spaniels. Liver-coloured, long, curly hair covers its whole body apart from its muzzle, chest and long, whip-like tail.

Temperament A bold and daring retriever with great character and power. Its coat is ideal for keeping it warm when working in cold waters. On first meeting, the dog may seem reserved but once it gets to know you it will become a faithful and friendly companion.

Suitability as a pet Ideal for the house-proud owner, it does not shed hair. It is good with children and other dogs. It loves open spaces and swimming. It responds to training but needs an experienced owner to be at its best. It is not particularly popular as a domestic dog.

The Irish Water Spaniel was renowned for its temperament and its stamina in the waters of the North Sea

Height 51–8 cm (20–3 in)
Weight 20–30 kg (45–65 lb)
Life span 12–14 years
Grooming * * *
Exercise * *
Town or Country C

Labrador Retriever

Reliable, courageous and diligent, the Labrador is an extrovert but easy-going dog renowned for its obedience, hard work and friendship.

Origins The Labrador came from Newfoundland where it was used to help the fishermen bring their catches ashore. In the nineteenth century, local landowners acquired some of the dogs from ships bringing salt cod to Poole, Dorset. Bred with other English sporting dogs, it became relied on first as a gundog then as an all-round working dog.

Appearance Stocky, with a broad head, powerful jaws and a strong neck, the Labrador is an immediately recognizable breed. Its coat is short and water resistant and it may be one of three colours: black, golden or chocolate.

Temperament Enormously adaptable and easily trained, the Labrador is one of the most reliable and steadfast breeds in the world. It has been successful as a police dog, a gundog, a canine mine detector and as a guide dog for the blind.

The gundog group

Suitability as a pet Perfectly suited to family life, patient, affectionate and loyal. It is responsive to training, is patient with children and loves exercise.

A sturdy breed, the Labrador loves its food and can be prone to excessive weight gain if not carefully watched

Height 54–7 cm (21.5–2.5 in)
Weight 25–34 kg (55–75 lb)
Life span 12–13 years
Grooming *
Exercise * *
Town or Country T/C

Sussex Spaniel

The rarest spaniel of all and the one with the longest history. Less than 500 of the breed exist in America today and it is unusual to see one at all in England.

Origins It was developed in the Sussex countryside to work as a gundog in thick undergrowth. An experienced hunter could distinguish the different tones in its voice and so tell what kind of animal was being tracked.

Appearance The most distinctive thing about this breed is its coat, which has a thick first layer and is always a rich golden-liver colour. Its head is broad with a quizzically wrinkled brow. It is heavy-boned and its short, strong legs allow it to get underneath thick brush.

Temperament The Sussex Spaniel takes life seriously and although a friendly dog, it can become aggressive when protecting its territory. Its occasionally obstinate character can frustrate the most patent of owners.

Suitability as a pet Not a good all-round pet although it has a gentle nature and is good with children. It is primarily a working dog, however, and is best suited to a country household.

The gundog group

Above The Sussex Spaniel has a thick weatherproof coat with feathering on the ears, legs and abdomen

Above Its soft, hazel eyes lend an irresistibly endearing expression

Height 38–41 cm (15–16 in)
Weight 18–23 kg (40–50 lb)
Life span 12–13 years
Grooming * *
Exercise * *
Town or Country C

Weimaraner

Nicknamed the 'grey ghost', the Weimaraner is an assertive, headstrong dog that excels in the field and, if firmly handled, can make a top-class companion.

Origins Its ancestors are believed to be bloodhounds and German short-haired pointers. Bred by the noblemen of the German court of Weimar to hunt large game such as boar, elk or deer, it later became a bird dog, used for retrieving waterfowl.

Appearance The coat is short and sleek and its colour ranges from mouse to silver grey. It has a powerful, muscular body with a deep chest for endurance and a noble head held high. Its eyes are a striking blue-grey or amber. The tail is usually docked. A rare version of the Weimaraner with a longer coat also exists.

Temperament Its handsome stance is mirrored in its personality, which is alert, fearless and obedient. It is graceful, strong-willed and intelligent.

Suitability as a pet Gentle with children but, due to its madcap nature, often hard to house-train. It needs a firm hand. The Weimaraner makes a great watchdog.

The gundog group

Above Exercise is a must for this this energetic and fun-loving breed

Above The Weimaraner is distinguished by its neat lines, short greyish coat and piercing blue or amber eyes

Height 56–69 cm (22–7 in)
Weight 32–9 kg (70–80 lb)
Life span 12–13 years
Grooming *
Exercise * * *
Town or Country T/C

The terrier group

Almost all the dogs in the terrier group originate from the British Isles. Their name comes from the Latin 'terra' or 'earth'. They were first bred for chasing down fox, rabbit or badger holes. Their short legs, flexible body and tough character made them ideal for the job.

Terriers are a relatively new breed of dog, the first written references to them being made in the sixteenth and seventeenth centuries. The earliest recognized breed was the Black-and-tan, a spirited terrier that would take on any form of vermin, and the English White. Burrowing underground meant the dogs had to be kept small – early fox terriers were carried in huntsmen's saddlebags until they were released to flush out the fox or to be in at the kill.

The dogs were used as ratters too, and during the Industrial Revolution they were employed not only in the country but also in factories and down the mines. They were also used for sport, frequently fighting in rat pits and against other dogs. Terriers and their descendants are characterized by their tenacity – they will not stand down in a fight and once they've bitten will not let go.

The terrier group

During the nineteenth century, breeders began to selectively breed terriers according to the kind of terrain in which they were to work. This resulted in the wide range of sizes and colours that exists today, from the Airedale down to the cairn. There are currently 29 different British terrier breeds. The larger breeds were not used for going to earth but specifically for chasing, capturing and killing. The mastiffs used for baiting larger animals were crossed with terriers to give a more aggressive dog, resulting in the bull terrier breeds.

What all terriers have in common, to a greater or lesser degree, is their character – feisty, energetic and often ready for a spat. Over the years, they have become domesticated and with the right training and early socialization with other dogs can make first-rate pets. They are extremely adaptable and find city life as much to their liking as life in the country. They love the noise and bustle of family life and, despite their sometimes small size, are dogs with tremendous character – entertaining, energetic and fun. Training is a must if their tendency to nip and yap is to be controlled. Recently the terrier has been used as a working dog again, being trained in underground rescue work.

Airedale Terrier

Known as the King of Terriers, the Airedale is the biggest of the group. It was trained to retrieve in otter, badger and wolf hunting.

Origins The breed was developed during the nineteenth century in the Aire valley in Yorkshire. Thought to be a cross between the Otter Hound and the old English Broken-haired Terrier, it was bred for its grit, intelligence and fighting ability.

Appearance A strong, confident-looking dog, it is well boned and squarely built. Its thick wiry coat is tan with a black saddle. Its face has a distinctive beard, moustache and eyebrows, with neat, folded ears.

Temperament This is a dog with a strong, outgoing personality and its intelligence needs to be harnessed if the best is to be got from it. It makes a good watchdog but has a tendency to brawl with other dogs if not controlled.

Suitability as a pet It is playful and protective of its family. It loves exercise and is a keen digger. Early socializing and training are essential to prevent general delinquency. Its coat needs daily brushing.

The terrier group

Right Though large for the group, the Airedale retains its terrier qualities

Left A well built, athletic dog that is recognisable by the friendly expression on its bearded face and its neat folded ears

Height 58–61 cm (22–4 in)
Weight 20–3 kg (44–50 lb)
Life span 13 years
Exercise **
Grooming ***
Town or Country T/C

Bedlington Terrier

It may look more like a lamb than a dog, but its gentle appearance hides a true terrier nature and it needs plenty of mental stimulation if it is to stay on the right side of trouble.

Origins During the nineteenth century, gypsies bred the Bedlington in Rothbury Forest, Northumbria. It is reputed to be a descendant of the Dandie Dinmont and the whippet, hence its speed and agility when it came to racing, rabbit catching and ratting.

Appearance A gentle-looking dog with a confident personality that shines through. Its unusual coat is either blue or sandy. It has a long neck and head, and long legs (from its whippet ancestry) with tucked-in loins.

Temperament Known for its tenacity and spirit, the Bedlington was once used in dog fighting and this tendency can surface when it is with other dogs.

Suitability as a pet Not as popular as a family pet as it once was. A feisty individual that needs plenty of stimulation and exercise to keep it out of mischief. Like its relatives, it loves digging. It can be obstinate but has an affectionate nature. Regular grooming is required.

The terrier group

Above The Bedlington's coat is thick and stands up from its skin. A fringe of hair is always left on the tip of its ears

Above The Bedlington may look like a lamb but it has the nature of a terrier

Height 38–43 cm (15–17 in)
Weight 8–10 kg (17–23 lb)
Life span 14–15 years
Exercise * *
Grooming * *
Town or Country T/C

Border Terrier

A tough, no-nonsense, rabbiting and badgering dog that also makes a big-hearted member of the family.

Origins Developed on the Scottish/Northumbrian borders in the eighteenth century, the Border Terrier is related to both the Dandie Dinmont and the Bedlington terrier – both terriers were originally from the same area. It was used as a hunting dog, as it could cope with the rough terrain and keep up with the hunt but was small enough to scramble down the tiniest rabbit or foxhole.

Appearance It has a distinctive otter-like head quite unlike that of other terriers. It has a sound, medium-sized body covered in a wiry coat that protects it from adverse weather conditions. The coat comes in a number of different colours, including red, wheaten, grizzle (grey) and tan or blue and tan.

Temperament A cheerful, friendly dog that is both smart and reliable. It is generally not quarrelsome though may pick a fight with another dog if not thoroughly socialized.

The terrier group

Suitability as a pet A great addition to the family, with its abundance of energy and lovable nature. Be prepared to be firm.

Right The Border Terrier has always been known for its gameness and working qualities

Left Bred as a working dog, it none the less makes a superb family pet which has enormous energy and is a lot of fun

Height 25–8 cm (10–11 in)
Weight 5–7 kg (11–15 lb)
Life span 13–14 years
Exercise * *
Grooming * *
Town or Country T/C

Bull Terrier

The Bull Terrier's striking appearance, with its slightly oval head and Roman nose, will appeal to those who want an intimidating watchdog as well as a pet with attitude.

Origins James Hinks was one of the men who played an important role in the development of the breed. In the mid-1800s, he crossed bulldogs with terriers to produce this superb fighting dog with great tenacity and agility.

Appearance Usually thought of as white, the bull terrier can be black, fawn, red or brindle, with some white on the head, neck or legs. The coat is short and flat. Packed with muscle, it stands solidly with its ears and tail erect.

Temperament The fighting tendencies have been bred out of the dog to provide a solid, even-tempered companion. It is good with people and enjoys exercise.

Suitability as a pet Provided it is properly trained, it can be a loyal and devoted friend. It gets on with children but should be watched when other dogs are around unless it has been thoroughly socialized. Once it gets its teeth into something, it can be hard to shake off.

The terrier group

Above Pricked ears,
a rounded nose and
a stubborn streak
characterize this breed

Above This lean power-packed
dog is nicknamed the Gladiator
of the Terriers because of its
unquenchable spirit

Height 53–6 cm (21–2 in)
Weight 24–8 kg (52–62 lb)
Life span 11–13 years
Exercise * *
Grooming *
Town or Country T/C

Cairn Terrier

Immortalized by Dorothy's dog Toto in *The Wizard of Oz*, the Cairn Terrier is among the most popular of the pet terriers, thanks to the combination of its fun-loving nature and engaging appearance.

Origins Thought to have originated in the Middle Ages on the Isle of Skye, where it was used to keep the rodent population down. It is the forerunner of both the Scottie and the West Highland white.

Appearance Small and compact and with bags of character. Its shaggy coat is weatherproof and usually brindled, but can range from cream and grey to wheaten, red and nearly black. Its sharp ears make it look alert and ready for anything.

Temperament These are frisky little dogs that are always on the lookout for something new to do. They thrive on attention and need to have time devoted to them. A typical terrier, it loves digging but also adds chewing and climbing into its bad points. It can be quite vocal, making it a good watchdog and an engaging communicator.

Suitability as a pet Definitely a 'people' dog. It will be steadfastly loyal to its owner, play happily with children and train easily. Although it is happy to take exercise, it doesn't require much to keep fit. It does need a little grooming to maintain that disreputable look.

Right This terrier is blessed with oodles of personality and a big heart

Above Cairns can be very territorial and will make good security dogs

Height 25–30 cm (10–12 in)
Weight 6–7 kg (13–16 lb)
Life span 14 years
Exercise *
Grooming *
Town or Country T/C

Dandie Dinmont Terrier

Named after a character that owned six of the dogs in Sir Walter Scott's novel *Guy Mannering*, the Dandie Dinmont neither looks nor behaves like a typical terrier.

Origins Bred in the Cheviot Hills as a hunting dog for otters, foxes and badgers, this was an animal renowned for its courageousness. Those days are long over and its reputation today is as a loyal and affable companion.

Appearance Its soulful eyes peer from a large head topped with a cap of hair. It has a double coat – a wiry topcoat with a softer coat beneath. The topcoat comes in two colours, mustard and pepper. It has a long back and short legs, the front ones slightly curved.

Temperament Intelligent and determined, this is a friendly, independent breed. Unlike its relations, it is not snappy or a digger, although its hunting instincts may surface if faced with a mouse or squirrel.

Suitability as a pet A great family dog that will stay calm in the face of provocation. Its territorial nature and deep bark make it an impressive watchdog. It needs little exercise but care must be taken not to overfeed it.

The terrier group

Right Its gentle eyes gaze from a large head covered with a fetching topknot of hair

Above Perhaps the most unusual looking of the terrier breed, the Dandie Dinmont also has a distinctive loud, deep bark

Height 20–8 cm (8–11 in)
Weight 8–11 kg (18–24 lb)
Life span 13–14 years
Exercise *
Grooming *
Town or Country T/C

Fox Terrier (smooth and wire)

Not nearly as popular as it used to be, the Fox Terrier – smooth or wire-haired – is an ancient breed that makes an extremely lively companion today.

Origins The origins of the breed are obscure but there is no doubt that fox terriers were used to flush out the fox towards the hounds after they had run it to ground. The wire and smooth varieties we know today were first recorded in the 1850s.

Appearance An alert dog, ready to stand its ground against anyone or anything that crosses it. Squarely built with legs and feet that make it look as if it is standing on tiptoe ready for the off. The smooth variety has a neat white coat with black or tan markings. The wire-haired variety has a harsh coat, white with a black saddle and other black or tan markings. It has distinctive eyebrows, moustache and beard, with longer hair on its legs and chest.

Temperament Strong-willed, occasionally stubborn, independent and always up for action. The wire variety can be snappy and wilful.

The terrier group

Suitability as a pet Needs persistent and careful training if it is to make a good family pet. It needs plenty of exercise and the wire variety needs regular grooming.

Above A neatly-proportioned dog which will stand up for itself against any challenger

Above The wire Fox Terrier has the same instincts as its smooth-coated relation but has a thick wiry coat

Height 38.5–9.5 cm (15 in)
Weight 7–8 kg (16–18 lb)
Life span 13–14 years
Exercise **
Grooming smooth */ wire ***
Town or Country C

Irish Terrier

An accomplished sporting dog that will retrieve on water and land. Nicknamed the 'red devil', it is more than happy to take on all-comers from the canine world.

Origins One of the oldest terriers developed in southern Ireland, the Irish Terrier is thought to be descended from the black-and-tan and wheaten terriers. It was originally used as a watchdog and ratter but during the Second World War proved its use as a messenger and sentinel.

Appearance A handsome dog, it has a dense, wiry coat that ranges from red to wheaten in colour. It looks a little like an Airedale, sporting a similar moustache and beard, but its coat is thinner.

Temperament A feisty creature that gets on famously with people but notoriously badly with other dogs. This is the archetypal terrier that loves activity, the thrill of the chase, digging and scrapping.

Suitability as a pet Needs to be socialized and trained firmly at a young age if it is not to cause problems as a pet. It will be fiercely devoted to its owner and make a good playmate for children, and an effective guard dog.

The terrier group

Above An intrepid character with a bright intelligence and playful nature

Below The Irish Terrier is as accomplished a retriever in the water as it is a hunter on land

Height 46–8 cm (18–19 in)
Weight 11–12 kg (25–7 lb)
Life span 13 years
Exercise * *
Grooming *
Town or Country T/C

Jack Russell Terrier

The Jack Russell is a close relative of the Parson Jack Russell, a slightly taller, wire-haired breed. The first was bred as a rat catcher, the second for its speed and agility in the field, where it pursued and flushed out quarry.

Origins Both breeds were named after the Rev. John Russell from Devonshire, reputedly a hard-drinking huntsman, who bred dogs small and flexible enough to bolt foxes out of their dens. Russell is said to have bought the founding dog of the breed from a milkman.

Appearance The Jack Russell is a small, smooth-coated muscular dog, usually white with black and/or tan markings. Its relative, the Parson Jack Russell, is taller, of similar colouring and has both smooth and wire coats.

Temperament Apart from the differences in size and coat, the characters of the two breeds are similar: rambunctious, fearless, lively and confident.

Suitability as a pet This is a very active dog with a layer of terrier aggression that makes co-existence with other pets problematic. It is a prodigious digger and barker too.

The terrier group

A bright eye and an alert personality make the Jack Russell a fun-loving playmate as well as a fearless hunter

Height: Jack Russell 25–6 cm (10–12 in);
Parson Jack Russell 28–38 cm (11–15 in)

Weight: Jack Russell 4–7kg (9–15 lb);
Parson Jack Russell 5–8 kg (12–18 lb)

Life span 13–14 years

Exercise * *

Grooming *

Town or Country T/C

Kerry Blue Terrier

Legend has it that deep in the mists of time a blue dog swam ashore from a foreign ship wrecked in Tralee Bay in Ireland. This dog was believed to be the original Irish Kerry blue: the national dog of Ireland.

Origins The breed originated in County Kerry, where it was used for hunting small game, retrieving from land and water, and herding cattle and sheep.

Appearance When born, Kerry Blue puppies have a black coat but this changes to blue when they are between nine months and two years old. The adult coat is much softer than that of other terriers and does not shed, making it a good dog for those with allergies to dog hair.

Temperament An elegant animal that enjoys strutting its stuff. It is full of life but, like almost all terriers, will scrap with another dog when it gets the chance. Otherwise it is a fun-loving, sociable animal.

Suitability as a pet Its temperament can be too fiery for some families. However, it does enjoy the companionship a family can offer and in exchange will provide loyalty, laughs and be a fierce security guard.

The terrier group

Above A solid, square looking dog that is trimmed to maintain its neat outlline

Below When trimmed, the Kerry Blue Terrier has a distinctive beard. It is a great all-rounder, having been used for hunting, herding and retrieving from land and water

Height 46–8 cm (18–19 in)
Weight 15–17 kg (33–7 lb)
Life span 14 years
Exercise **
Grooming ***
Town or Country T/C

Scottish Terrier

One of the best-known Highland terriers, this cheerful breed has become firmly associated with its country of origin, appearing on all manner of clothes, advertisements and food packaging.

Origins The 'Scottie' was developed along with other terriers to hunt vermin. It is thought to have been bred in Aberdeenshire during the mid-nineteenth century.

Appearance Short-legged but surprisingly strong and agile. It has a thick, rough coat of varied colours: steel, iron-grey, black, sandy, wheaten or brindle. It has a soft undercoat but what distinguishes it most from the other Highland terriers is its prodigious beard.

Temperament Independent, stubborn and wilful on occasions, the 'Scottie' definitely has a mind of its own. It barks, digs and enjoys wandering off alone.

Suitability as a pet This small, dour dog can run rings round a family if it isn't well trained. It has an aggressive streak so is not ideal for a family with young children.

The terrier group

A thick-set, sturdy small dog with loads of personality, the Scottie is noted for its thick beard and long eyebrows. Despite its size, it is very active and will rise to the occasion when provoked

Height 25.5–8 cm (10–11 in)
Weight 8.5–10.5 kg (19–23 lb)
Life span 13–14 years
Exercise **
Grooming ***
Town or Country T/C

Staffordshire Bull Terrier

A particularly popular breed with men who may feel its muscular prowess reflects something of their own. However, this is also a friendly family dog that will vigorously see off intruders.

Origins Originating in Staffordshire, this was a breed developed for bull baiting, dog fighting and ratting. When these activities were eventually banned by the mid-1800s, the Staffordshire bull terrier became a companion and show dog.

Appearance A solid, muscular dog that stands full square. Its short coat comes in red, fawn, black, blue, brindle or a combination of any of these colours with white.

Temperament Intelligent and courageous, this is the Jekyll-and-Hyde of the dog world. It usually behaves like an angel with its family and their friends but show it another dog and immediately the situation changes. It has an aggressive streak that is hard to quell, even though selective breeding has gone some way towards this.

The terrier group

Suitability as a pet Great with human beings and a devoted family member but a ferocious fighter with other dogs. Early socialization and training are essential if its instincts are to be curbed.

Originally bred for its fighting power, the Staffordshire Bull Terrier needs to be carefully controlled particularly with other dogs

Height 36–41 cm (14–16 in)
Weight 11–17 kg (24–38 lb)
Life span 11–12 years
Exercise **
Grooming *
Town or Country T/C

West Highland White Terrier

The 'Westie' makes a perfect companion. Friendly, talkative and alert, it is a spunky, active little dog that makes a devoted and loyal pet.

Origins The West Highland Terrier comes from the same Highland background as the Scottish terriers, cairns and Dandie Dinmonts. It was selectively bred in the 1800s by the Poltalloch family in Argyllshire, Scotland, and known both as the Poltalloch terrier and the Roseneath terrier.

Appearance Less stocky than the Scottie, with whom it is often paired. Its tough double coat is always white and therefore needs some looking after to stop it looking dirty. It has small upright ears, bright slightly sunken eyes and a perky stance.

Temperament This is a self-confident little dog with lots of character, making it good company. The Westie may be small but it is intelligent, active and entertaining. This is an extremely adaptable dog that will make itself equally at home in the country or in a high-rise apartment.

Suitability as a pet It can be as stubborn as the other terrier breeds so early training is essential but it learns fast and responds well to praise. Westies are good with children but make equally good pets for the elderly, as they need little exercise and have buckets of charm.

The West Highland White is one of the most popular terriers with its endearing, extrovert character and gentle, friendly nature

Height 25–8 cm (10–11 in)
Weight 7–10 kg (15–22 lb)
Life span 14 years
Exercise *
Grooming **
Town or Country T/C

The working group

The working group is made up of dogs which have been trained to perform specific work particularly guard duties or search and rescue work. Some breeds such as the Rottweiler, Doberman or Boxer have more recently been trained to work with the police or military. These dogs are noted for their heroism in the face of danger, their endurance and stamina. They are intelligent animals that are quick to learn and immensely capable. Their size may make them unsuitable as pets for the average family but, properly trained, they can be relied upon for unswerving loyalty and companionship.

Many of these breeds share a common ancestry in the great mastiffs of the Roman times which were bred specifically for their size, bravery and strength, qualities which could be harnessed in times of war. As the Romans travelled across Europe, their dogs crossed with native breeds to produce some of the mountain dogs we know today which are still used to guard, search and rescue, and to pull carts or sledges as well as making good household pets.

The working group

Dogs have very strong territorial instincts and have been used for centuries to guard property. Once the large mastiff breeds defended their masters' farms or homesteads, now they are also effectively used on building sites, within factories and shops as well. These tend to be the larger breeds which are as intimidating as they are loud. Originally, dogs that guarded the home were kept outside but now they are more often than not kept indoors. Their protective instinct is deeply ingrained so, when taken as family pets, they need to be trained carefully from an early age so that they do not behave aggressively towards strangers, children or other dogs.

The exuberant Boxer is a versatile dog which does well in obedience and agility tests and has worked successfully with the police and military

Bernese Mountain Dog

A splendid creature that remains a working dog in its native Switzerland but that will also willingly adapt to a life of domestic bliss. Sufficiently fussed over, it will become a devoted companion.

Origins Swiss mountain dogs may be divided into four breeds, all of which are believed to derive from the mastiffs brought to the country in Roman times. The Bernese Mountain Dog was a farm worker, used in the main for herding cattle, pulling carts and guarding property.

Appearance A huge, powerful dog that is surprisingly agile for its size. Most notable is its thick, shiny black coat with chestnut markings above the eyes, on the cheeks, legs and under the tail, and the distinctive white blaze on its face, the white cross on its chest and its white paws.

Temperament A gentle, well-mannered dog that enjoys its work and responds intelligently to training. It will readily compete in agility trials as it can search and rescue or herd cattle.

Suitability as a pet It has a great affinity with children and can become a valued member of the family. However, you shouldn't underestimate its need to be occupied – regular daily exercise and other training regimes are a must to keep it out of trouble.

Originally a cattle herder and cart puller, the Bernese Mountain Dog also makes an affectionate and stalwart companion

Height 58–70 cm (23–7.5 in)
Weight 40–4 kg (87–90 lb)
Life span 8–10 years
Exercise ***
Grooming **
Town or Country C

Boxer

The Boxer is a vibrant, rambunctious dog that has a great love of life. Its extrovert character can get it into trouble but its charm will always come to the rescue.

Origins The boxer's roots are in Germany, where it is a descendant of the Bullenbeiser, which was used initially for hunting wild boar and deer or for bull baiting, and then later as a guard dog.

Appearance A compact, muscular dog with a distinctive squashed face and wrinkled brow. Its short, glossy coat comes in fawn or brindle, with white markings. It is extremely athletic with powerful hindquarters that ensure its fluid movement.

Temperament Its exuberance can get the better of it so make sure your Boxer knows who is boss from an early age. Without firm training, its recalcitrant nature and self-assurance can overwhelm its other good points.

Suitability as a pet A tremendously good-natured dog that will adapt well to children and strangers. It does need exercise and play to satisfy both the curious and energetic sides of its nature.

The working group

Above The Boxer is distinguished by its particular body shape and squashed face

Above This is a dog that loves action and which will stand up for itself when challenged

Height 53–63 cm (21–5 in)
Weight 25–32 kg (55–70 lb)
Life span 11–12 years
Exercise * * *
Grooming *
Town or Country T/C

Bull Mastiff

A massive, intimidating exterior belies the essentially even temperament and loyal nature of the Bull Mastiff. It is a tolerant animal whose natural instinct is to scare off strangers rather than actually to hunt them down or attack them.

Origins The Bull Mastiff is a British breed developed by crossing the Mastiff with the Bulldog. It was a breed largely used by gamekeepers to intimidate poachers. It was also used as a tracking dog.

Appearance Although smaller and more compact than its close relative the Mastiff, the Bull Mastiff is a large, powerful dog that it would be wise not to cross. It has a short, hard coat that can be brindle, fawn or red. Its head is reminiscent of that of the bulldog but with a less squashed nose.

Temperament The Bull Mastiff is an even-tempered and loyal creature that makes a perfect watchdog. Its intelligence can be matched by a stubborn streak, which may make it difficult to train except by an experienced owner.

Suitability as a pet Despite appearances, the Bull Mastiff is happy around children, but training can be problematic for the inexperienced. It has a huge appetite and needs plenty of space for exercise. It is one of the great droolers, which may put off some potential owners.

Despite its massive size, it has a gentle nature and can make a devoted companion

Height 64–9 cm (25–7 in)
Weight 41–59 kg (90–130 lb)
Life span 10–12 years
Exercise * *
Grooming *
Town or Country T/C

Doberman Pinscher

Specifically bred to be the quintessential guard dog, the Doberman is not to be trifled with. Given the right training, though, it can become a loyal and affectionate companion.

Origins During the 1870s a German tax collector, Herr Louis Dobermann, wanted an intimidating dog for protection. By crossing various breeds – the Rottweiler, German Pinscher, Manchester Terrier (black-and-tan), Weimaraner and English Greyhound – he produced this sleek and fearless guard dog.

Appearance An athletic, well-muscled dog that looks proud and unassailable. Its short gleaming coat is usually black but does come in black and tan, blue-grey, red and fawn as well. The muzzle, chest, legs and feet are tan. Its head is wedge-shaped with ears that may or may not have been cropped (illegal in the UK and Australia).

Temperament It is intelligent, loyal and protective, needing regular, vigorous exercise to prevent neurotic or destructive behaviour. Once known for its ill temper, the Doberman has become more reliable through selective breeding, but still needs to know who is in charge.

Suitability as a pet They can make devoted pets but should be firmly trained from an early age. Although their aggression may be bred out of them, they should not be left unsupervised with children.

The Doberman Pinscher was bred to be a guard dog and has a reputation for ferocity

Height 65–9 cm (25.5–7 in)
Weight 30–40 kg (66–88 lb)
Life span 12 years
Exercise * * *
Grooming *
Town or Country T/C

Great Dane

Chaucer referred to a similar type of dog in the 1200s. Since then this splendid breed has become the national dog of Germany.

Origins The Great Dane comes not from Denmark but from Germany, where it was used to hunt wild boar and stags and as a war dog. Its origins go back to the mastiffs introduced to Europe by the Romans, possibly crossed with some greyhound to give it added speed and elegance.

Appearance A dignified animal with an elegant loping gait. Its muscular frame includes a deep chest and long legs with powerful hindquarters. The male is considerably larger than the female. The coat is short and sleek in five different colours: fawn, brindle, blue, black and harlequin (white with irregular patches of black or another dark colour).

Temperament Kindly, faithful and dependable, the Great Dane has a nobility of temperament that suits its appearance. Its size and bark may scare off intruders but in fact it loves people.

Suitability as a pet It can be a wonderful family member but needs firm training, since it is too big an animal to be undisciplined. Small children may accidentally get knocked over in its wake.

A real gentle giant, the dignified Great Dane needs plenty of houseroom

Height 71–6 cm (28–30 in)
Weight 46–54 kg (100–20 lb)
Life span 9–10 years
Exercise * * *
Grooming *
Town or Country T/C

Newfoundland

The Newfoundland is legendary for its prowess in the water and its ability to rescue people from drowning. Perhaps the most famous Newfoundland is Nana, the children's nurse in *Peter Pan*.

Origins Thought to be native to North America, where its ancestor was the greater St John's dog, the Newfoundland has played a distinguished part in Canada's fishing industry. It would haul the nets to and from the boats and rescue any men who fell overboard. It was equally at home on land, where it pulled loaded carts and sleds.

Appearance A great big dog with a thick coarse double coat that was developed to keep it warm on land and at sea. It can be black, brown or black and white. This last variation is known as a Landseer, after its appearance in a painting by Sir Edwin Landseer. It has specially webbed feet to help it swim.

Temperament A gentle, patient dog, it has a sweet temperament. It is strong and courageous, which makes it a good working dog. It loves swimming.

Suitability as a pet Dangerously seductive as a puppy, the Newfoundland does require a lot of hard work. It is big, slobbery and has a coat that sheds. If you are not house-proud and have plenty of space, a Newfoundland will make a marvellous pet – gentle with children and utterly devoted.

The Newfoundland is a huge bundle of fun. It loves exercise, particularly in water

Height 66–71 cm (26–8 in)
Weight 50–68 kg (110–50 lb)
Life span 9–11 years
Exercise * * *
Grooming * * *
Town or Country C

Rottweiler

The Rottweiler's aggressive tendencies have earned it a bad press. However, with consistent training and firm handling it can be a responsive and reliable companion.

Origins With Roman mastiffs as its forebears, the Rottweiler was developed in Rottweil, a town in southern Germany originally founded by the Romans themselves. The dogs were used to herd cattle to the butchers and to pull their carts. Later, their intelligence and strength were utilized by the German police force.

Appearance A hefty dog that seems solid muscle, it has a deep, broad chest and powerful hindquarters. The short, smooth coat is always black with rusty markings on the eyebrows, muzzle, chest and legs. The tail is docked short.

Temperament If the dog is properly trained and socialized, a well-bred Rottweiler will be intelligent, calm and confident. It responds well to training and likes human contact. It can seem reserved or aloof and may show its temper with other dogs. It needs plenty of exercise.

Suitability as a pet This is not a dog to suit everyone. With an owner who is sufficiently committed to training and exercising it, however, the Rottweiler can make a rewarding and loyal partner.

Below The Rottweiler is a heavy dog, packed with muscle. It is very intelligent but needs a firm owner

Above It is essential that the powerful nature of the dog is checked by good training

Height 58–69 cm (23–7 in)
Weight 41–50 kg (90–110 lb)
Life span 11–12 years
Exercise ***
Grooming *
Town or Country T/C

St Bernard

Traditionally pictured with a brandy cask at its neck as it combs the alpine mountains in search of missing people, the St Bernard has a reputation as a rescue dog that is second-to-none.

Origins Descended from the original Roman mastiffs, the St Bernard was named after Bernard de Menthon, an eleventh-century monk who established a hospice on a remote alpine pass. The dogs were initially brought up as companions for the monks but by the mid-1800s their status as rescue dogs had been established.

Appearance A great hulk of a dog, its dense coat can be medium- or short-haired and either orange, red-brindle or brown-brindle with white. A big dog in every way, its skull and jaws are huge, it neck muscular and its chest deep for stamina. It has a kindly expression and an acute sense of smell.

Temperament A benevolent, trustworthy animal that needs to be thoroughly trained before it gets too big and too strong to control. It is steadfast, affectionate and placid.

Suitability as a pet It does get on with children but is demanding in terms of space and feeding costs. Not to be taken on as a pet without considerable thought.

Right A massive dog famed for its rescue missions in snowy landscapes

Above The St Bernard is big-boned, with a huge skull and drooping lower lips which tend to drool

Height 61–71 cm (24–8 in)
Weight 50–91 kg (110–200 lb)
Life span 9–11 years
Exercise ***
Grooming ***
Town or Country C

Samoyed

The Samoyed's intelligent, smiling face reflects its good-humoured, friendly nature. Originally from Siberia, the breed has wound up as a popular if demanding pet all over the world.

Origins The Samoyed people of Siberia were nomadic and used their dogs to herd reindeer, pull sledges, guard flocks and provide warmth. The breed was introduced to the West at the end of the nineteenth century, when it was simultaneously being used for polar expeditions.

Appearance A solid, graceful dog that is capable of great stamina. The coat is thick and usually white but can be varying shades of biscuit or fawn. Its expression is alert, its eye rims and lips black, its ears pricked up and tail curled tightly round. Its feet are flat and hairy enough to cope with walking on ice.

Temperament The Samoyed is an independent animal that can be extremely stubborn. However, it loves human company and if training is carried out from an early age it can become an affectionate and loyal companion.

Suitability as a pet Handled badly, the Samoyed can be wilful, aggressive to other dogs and resistant to training. Its coat sheds heavily and needs regular grooming. But for a dedicated owner, it can be a great family pet, good with children and very playful.

The Samoyed has been dubbed the Laughing Cavalier of the canine world thanks to its friendly expression

Height 46–56 cm (18–22 in)
Weight 23–30 kg (50–66 lb)
Life span 12 years
Exercise * * *
Grooming * * *
Town or Country T/C

Siberian Husky

Famed for its speed and endurance, which allows it to cover vast tracts of snow-covered landscape, the Husky is tolerant of humans but does not always make an ideal pet.

Origins The Siberian Husky was once used by the Chukchi people of the extreme northeastern part of Siberia to pull sledges, herd reindeer and guard property. Fur traders took the huskies to America at the beginning of the twentieth century, where they are now used for sledge racing and as companions. Huskies are frequently used on polar expeditions.

Appearance A strong, athletic dog, the Siberian Husky is lean and rather like a wolf to look at. Its mask and chest are usually white but the rest of its warm coat comes in almost any colour. Unusually, its eyes can be of any colour too, or sometimes even two different colours.

Temperament The Husky is tireless and has an unending appetite for pulling sledges. It is alert, intelligent and tractable, wanting only to be friendly and enjoying any work it may be put to.

Suitability as a pet It is adaptable towards its surroundings but can be hard to train. An experienced owner is a must. Without sufficient exercise, it may become destructive. However, it is an affectionate animal that can also deter burglars.

A typical spitz-type dog which has been bred for pulling sledges and wants to do little else

Height 51–60 cm (20–3.5 in)
Weight 16–27 kg (35–60 lb)
Life span 11–13 years
Exercise ***
Grooming **
Town or Country C

The pastoral (herding) group

The pastoral group includes dogs that have helped man for centuries, gathering, herding and protecting cattle, sheep, reindeer and other livestock. They range in size from the Collie to the Corgi and use a variety of techniques to achieve their task. The tenacious Corgi herds cattle by nipping at their heels while the Border Collie can keep his charges still with a mesmerising stare. Their highly strong protective instinct has developed because they identify with the group they are minding and will defend it ferociously if necessary.

Many years ago, dogs used for guarding small flocks of sheep or herds of cattle against wolves or poachers began to develop their skills as they were used to round up the animals and bring in any stragglers. Gradually, as the numbers of livestock increased and the amount of land they covered became greater, so the dogs were trained to move the animals from one grazing place to another. Herding involves actions similar to hunting but these dogs have had the killing instinct bred out of them. They have thick protective weatherproof coats

The pastoral group

*The Cardigan Welsh Corgi
has been used as a guard dog,
hunter and cattle drover*

which enable them to spend long periods of time out in the worst conditions.

Herding dogs can make great pets but they have high energy levels, requiring both exercise and stimulation if they are not to become bored. If they do, then neurotic or destructive behaviour is a common result. Their herding instinct is so strong that, if they are not required to work for a living, they will tend to round up their owners particularly if there are children in the family. They are generally alert, lively animals which can attain a high level of obedience or agility training. They are extremely motivated and can be seen always watching their master, anticipating their next command. With sufficient attention and exercise they can make extremely rewarding companions.

Bearded Collie

An enthusiastic and hard worker, the Bearded Collie's appealing expression and boundless energy are qualities that are hard to resist.

Origins Thought to have descended from the Polish Lowland Sheepdog and Komondor (a powerful ancient Hungarian breed), it was bred to be a working sheepdog that would look after the flock, even when the shepherd might be far away. It was recognized by The Kennel Club (UK) in 1959 and has since gone on to win the hearts of dog lovers all over the world.

Appearance An athletic, medium-sized dog with a harsh, long coat that may be either grey, red, blue or sandy, but which always has white on the head, brisket and lower legs. It resembles an Old English sheepdog but has a long tail.

Temperament A disciplined dog with great endurance whose temperament can range from high-spirited and bold to gentle and more laid-back. Bearded Collies get on well with other dogs and sometimes give way to their herding instincts.

Suitability as a pet They are vigorous, enthusiastic dogs that love to be part of a family. They need stimulation, exercise and company if they are not to become frustrated and bored. They do need regular grooming.

Bred to be a farm dog, the Bearded Collie has become a popular pet. Agile, intelligent and fun

Height 51–6 cm (20–2 in)
Weight 18–27 kg (40–60 lb)
Life span 12–13 years
Exercise * * *
Grooming * * *
Town or Country T/C

Border Collie

Eager to please, agile and a born worker, the Border Collie is known first and foremost for its excellence as a sheepdog and in obedience trials.

Origins Bred to work in the hilly Scottish border country, the Border Collie has the speed and stamina required to round up sheep or cattle and move the flock to different pastures or to shelter. It is one of the few breeds of dog that is still used to carry out its original function.

Appearance Usually black and white, the collie has quite a long coat to help it deal with the Scottish winters. It is an athletic dog that can move swiftly and is able to creep close to the ground when required. Its most famous characteristic is its beady eye, which is relies on to intimidate the sheep and to watch its master for its next instruction.

Temperament Hard-working and with an active mind that always needs something to do. If it is not sufficiently occupied, its behaviour may become aggressive or destructive.

Suitability as a pet As long as it has plenty to do, the Border Collie will be a happy pet, affectionate towards its family and willing to play endless games of fetch. If bored, it can become a problem.

The Border Collie is a natural in obedience and agility competitions but it really excels at herding sheep

Height 46–54 cm (18–21 in)
Weight 14–22 kg (30–49 lb)
Life span 12–14 years
Exercise * *
Grooming * *
Town or Country C

Briard

The Briard is the French equivalent of the Old English sheepdog in appearance and has been used for centuries to guard and herd livestock.

Origins This is a breed that has been around for a long time. It can be seen on ancient French tapestries depicting the Emperor Charlemagne. The Briard was originally bred as a shepherd's dog but during the First World War soldiers returned home with stories of the dog's bravery as a message carrier, patrol dog and wagon-puller.

Appearance A strong dog with all the power necessary for herding. It looks rugged with its long, shaggy coat that comes in a variety of colours. Its large head is covered in hair but this does not impede the sharpness of its eye. It has double dew claws (the first digit on a dog's paw, that is not used for walking) on its hind legs.

Temperament A kindly, intelligent dog that will respond to training. It is energetic and fun-loving, if occasionally timid, with a disposition to take control if given half a chance.

Suitability as a pet Despite its appealing personality and seductive appearance, the Briard is not necessarily an easy pet. It needs an experienced owner who can control its natural herding and guarding instincts. If properly trained and socialized, however, it can be a well-adjusted, obedient member of the household.

A lively, intelligent dog that can be difficult to train. It needs careful attention if its coat is to look tidy

Height 57–69 cm (23–7 in)
Weight 33.5–4.5 kg (74–6 lb)
Life span 11–13 years
Exercise * *
Grooming * *
Town or Country T/C

Cardigan Welsh Corgi

According to Celtic mythology, the Corgi was a gift from the woodland fairies, whose harness marks can still be seen on their coats.

Origins There are records of the Cardigan Welsh Corgi dating back to 1200 BC. They are believed to have basset or dachshund blood. They became herding dogs to drive cattle to market or to fresh pastures by nipping at their heels. They would also guard the herd as well as the farmhouse and children.

Appearance A small but heavy dog with short, sturdy legs. Its short, wiry coat comes in any colour. It has a fox-like head with large, upright ears. Its muscular neck sits on a long body that has a full, well-coated tail.

Temperament Because they herd cattle by snapping at their heels, corgis can instinctively nip if not trained. Otherwise they are faithful, lively, fun-loving companions that, despite appearances, are agile enough to avoid the kick of a cow. Their guarding instincts are well developed – meaning they make effective and noisy watchdogs.

Suitability as a pet Not good with children as they can be snappy. They can be hard to train and aggressive to other dogs.

Corgis were also known as 'heelers' because of the way they herded cattle by nipping at their heels

Height 27–32 cm (10.5–12.5 in)
Weight 11–17 kg (25–38 lb)
Life span 12–14 years
Exercise * *
Grooming * *
Town or Country T/C

Collie (Rough and Smooth)

The Rough Collie shot to world stardom as the Lassie of book, film and TV fame. Once used primarily as a herding dog, it is now predominantly used as a companion or a show dog.

Origins Bred to herd sheep in the sometimes bleak Scottish hill country, the collie only became popular as a companion after Queen Victoria owned one. Its reputation increased further after its Hollywood success as Lassie.

Appearance The two types of collie differ only because of their coat; the Rough Collie is long-haired and the Smooth Collie short-haired. The coat comes in one of four basic colours: sable and white, tricolour (black, white and tan), blue merle and white. Its expression is alert, intelligent and appealing.

Temperament A very friendly dog that learns quickly. It can be reserved with strangers and, with its fierce bark, makes a good watchdog. If not carefully trained, its bark can become a persistent problem. The smooth-coat is often of a more nervous disposition.

Suitability as a pet The collie is a highly obedient dog that will be protective of and kind to children, especially if it has grown up with them. It needs regular exercise and grooming.

Above The Smooth Collie is the more active dog and requires greater exercise than his long-haired relation

Above The Rough Collie is the more glamorous of the pair and the more popular

Height 51–61 cm (20–4 in)
Weight 18–30 kg (40–66 lb)
Life span 12–13 years
Exercise ***
Grooming ***
Town or Country C

German Shepherd Dog (Alsatian)

A splendidly versatile dog that has been trained for the police, the military, as a search-and-rescue dog, a sniffer dog, a guard dog and a guide dog, among other things.

Origins In the early 1900s a German cavalry officer, Max von Stephanitz, instituted a breeding programme that crossed the lines of local herding and guard dogs. The new breed rose in popularity after the First World War, when tales of its heroism at the front, working with the Red Cross and for the police, were brought home.

Appearance A rugged, proud-looking animal whose intelligence shines in its eyes. Its coat is medium or long-haired and in a variety of colours, most frequently black with tan, fawn or grey markings. The white and cream versions are decried by some fans.

Temperament A clever, self-confident animal that at best has a pleasant, trustworthy character and that is easy to train, obedient and reliable. It can be aggressive towards other dogs and may require firm handling if the best is to be got from it.

Suitability as a pet It is important to check the dog's breeding. A sound, well-trained Alsatian makes a first-class companion that will be protective of its family and home. It is important that the owner is committed to the dog and handles it firmly.

Right Originally a herding dog, the German Shepherd has since embraced a range of different skills

Above These dogs are steady-natured and respond well to training

Height 55–66 cm (22–6 in)
Weight 34–43 kg (75–95 lb)
Life span 12–13 years
Exercise * * *
Grooming * *
Town or Country T/C

Old English Sheepdog

A happy-go-lucky extrovert of a dog who has changed from being a hard-working sheep and cattle herder into a fashionable domestic dog whose popularity was increased by its use in TV advertising.

Origins It is thought that the Old English Sheepdog may have derived from continental herding dogs such as the briard. In the nineteenth century, it began to be bred selectively as a sheep and cattle herding dog. Its tail was originally docked to mark it out as a herding dog so that it would be tax-exempt.

Appearance Its docked tail earned it the name 'bobtail'. Its big, square head has a short muzzle and dark eyes and is set on a strong neck. Its shoulders stand lower than its loins. The coat is thick and shaggy and usually either grey, blue or blue merle, sometimes with white markings.

Temperament An exuberant companion that can be more like a bull in a china shop. It is intelligent, loves people and is a pacifist, though one whose herding instincts may get the upper hand.

Suitability as a pet A wonderful family pet if you can cope with its energy, size and grooming. It will bond with the entire family and will love playing with everyone. It is the sheepdog's overwhelming affection rather than any aggression that needs tempering early on.

A wonderful family pet but one that demands a great deal of time in terms of exercise and grooming

Height 56–61 cm (22–4 in)
Weight 29.5–30.5 kg (65–7 lb)
Life span 12–13 years
Exercise * * *
Grooming * * *
Town or Country T/C

Pembroke Welsh Corgi

The Pembroke is the better known of the two breeds of corgi, thanks to the members of the British royal family, who have long been devoted to them as family pets and are frequently seen in their company.

Origins The breed developed later than the Cardigan Corgi. It may be the result of crosses between the Cardigans and the Norwegian vallhund, which was brought to Wales by the Vikings. Others say it may have been brought by Flemish weavers invited to Britain by Henry I. Pembroke Corgis were used to herd cattle, hunt, guard farms and as companions.

Appearance Smaller and less nimble than its Cardigan relation, the Pembroke has a double coat that is usually red with white markings but can be sable, fawn or black and tan. It has a foxy head and a strong, muscular body. It can be born without a tail or its tail may be docked.

Temperament This is a feisty bundle of energy that is unafraid of the cattle it herds, even to the extent of nipping them on the nose if they dare to charge it. An active, outgoing breed that enjoys relaxing too.

The pastoral group

Suitability as a pet The tendency to nip has been almost completely bred out of the Pembroke, which means it makes a better family pet than the Cardigan. If trained properly from an early age it can become an obedient and friendly pet with modest demands.

Pembroke Corgis have become known for being favourites of the English royal family

Height 25–31 cm (10–12 in)
Weight 10–12 kg (20–6 lb)
Life span 12–14 years
Exercise *
Grooming *
Town or Country T/C

Portuguese Water Dog

A powerful swimmer, this dog has a history of helping fishermen with their catches, while on land it has been used to hunt rabbit. It can make a loyal companion.

Origins This breed was held as almost sacred along the coast of the Algarve. Also known as the Portuguese Fishing Dog, it was used to take messages between boats, herd fish, find lost fishing tackle and stand on the bow of a ship, using its bark as a foghorn. It probably came to the UK with the Spanish Armada in 1588.

Appearance Similar to the Standard Poodle (see page 182), this is a robust dog with a thick, wavy coat that does not shed hair. It is brown or black and usually clipped in the lion clip (pictured) or the retriever clip (entire coat clipped to a length of one-inch, following the outline of the dog). Both clips leave a plume at the end of the tail. The water dog has webbed feet to help it swim.

Temperament An exuberant and energetic dog, it needs firm handling due to its obstinate streak. It thrives on training and human contact and, while a loyal, fun-loving companion, it can be tough and independent.

Suitability as a pet It can be a good family dog but it is demanding. If its natural high spirits are not channelled into regular exercise and obedience training it will quickly assume the upper hand.

The Portuguese Water Dog originated as a fishing dog and is still clipped traditionally to free its back legs for swimming

Height 43–57 cm (17–22.5 in)
Weight 16–25 kg (35–55 lb)
Life span 12–14 years
Exercise ***
Grooming ***
Town or Country C

Shetland Sheepdog

The 'Sheltie' has all the instincts of a working dog but today is known only as a family dog. It is particularly popular in Britain, America and Japan.

Origins The breed probably derives as a cross between the rough collie and native dogs of the Shetland Isles. The islands were a harsh environment cut off from the mainland which meant that the dogs were not widely known until the beginning of the twentieth century, when the breed was first recognized by the English and American Kennel Clubs.

Appearance A Rough Collie in miniature, it has a pointed face that can tilt enquiringly to one side. Its topcoat is long and straight and comes in sable, tricolour, blue merle, black and white, and black and tan. It has a very thick undercoat that needs regular grooming.

Temperament The Sheltie is an extremely intelligent, responsive little dog that reacts quickly to training. It has a natural instinct as a guard dog, which makes it invaluable. It is active and loves running and jumping. It is docile and devoted.

Suitability as a pet It reacts better with older children than young but loves to be part of the family. It can be a prodigious barker and the bark can be difficult to control. Regular grooming is a must.

The Shetland Sheepdog has a coat that needs thorough and regular grooming

Height 35–7 cm (14–15 in)
Weight 6–7 kg (14–16 lb)
Life span 13–14 years
Exercise * *
Grooming * * *
Town or Country T/C

The toy group

Toy dogs have existed for thousands of years. They were bred from larger dogs to produce pets that could be easily held and cared for. They were born to keep their owners warm and give them undiluted love and companionship.

They are first recorded in the Far East, where the Pekingese was one of the earliest breeds of 'sleeve dog', carried around and pampered by Chinese empresses. The Pekingese's counterpart in Japan was the Japanese Chin. These were two of various small dogs that graced the imperial courts over the years. Eventually they were brought to the West by traders and became the progenitors of many of the toy breeds that are so popular today.

By the sixteenth and seventeenth centuries, toy dogs had become favourites among the ladies of the royal courts and aristocracies of Europe. They were easily transportable and provided much needed warmth when travelling or in draughty places. They were a status symbol denoting their owners' wealth and position in society: King Charles Spaniels were popular in the English courts of Charles I and Charles II; Queen Alexandra supported the

Japanese Chin; the Papillon was the favourite breed of Henri II of France, Marie Antoinette and Madame de Pompadour. Some of the breeds, such as the Affenpinscher, the Griffon Bruxellois and the Yorkshire Terrier, also made excellent ratters, while others, such as the Pomeranian and Pekingese, made good watchdogs.

Today, the toy dogs are, without exception, ideal for an apartment dweller or someone who wants companionship without having to provide much in the way of exercise. However, it is important to remember that although these dogs may be diminutive their personality is not. Breeds such as the chihuahua or the Yorkshire Terrier are fiercely protective and don't back down easily. Fortunately, they are small enough to be lifted out of the way of trouble. Other problems associated with larger dogs, such as shedding, exercise and cost, are all minimized with a toy breed. Some of them, however, do require considerable time and effort invested in their grooming. They may be obstinate when it comes to training but their size means they can be easily controlled. Most are good with children but not suitable to be involved in the rough and tumble of family life, simply because of their physique.

Affenpinscher

This is a mischievous-looking dog the name of which means 'monkey-like terrier'. Its comical appearance endears it to its owners who enjoy its fun-loving, entertaining character.

Origins The affenpinscher's origins are lost in history. It appears in German artwork from the sixteenth century onwards and was probably bred from a cross of Pug-like breeds from Asia and local pinschers. It became an impressive ratter and vermin-catcher. In France it is known as the 'diablotin moustachu' or the 'moustached devil'.

Appearance There is no question that the affenpinscher most resembles a monkey. Its sparky personality shines through its bright eyes and its coarse coat is always untidy and almost always black, although occasionally there is some grey. Its tail has short hair and is usually carried erect.

Temperament A game little dog that is fearless when confronting intruders. It is alert, inquisitive and may have a stubborn streak.

Suitability as a pet The Affenpinscher makes a loyal, affectionate pet, although its obstinacy can make it difficult to train and some have a tendency to snap. It needs little exercise and makes an excellent watchdog.

Unmistakeable in appearance, the Affenpinscher is a feisty, affectionate little creature

Height 25–30 cm (10–12 in)
Weight 3–3.5 kg (7–8 lb)
Life span 14–15 years
Exercise *
Grooming *
Town or Country T/C

Bichon Frisé

A brilliant-white powder puff of a dog with button black eyes. Gregarious and loves to be the centre of attention.

Origins The precise origins of this breed are unclear but it is likely that it was introduced to the island of Tenerife by the Spaniards. Then known as the Tenerife terrier, it was taken to Europe by foreign traders. By the sixteenth century it was a court favourite in France.

Appearance Bichons are always white although puppies may be touched with buff or cream. The coat is fine and curly and the body is slightly longer than it is high, with the tail curled over the back. This dog moves with a confident, lively trot.

Temperament An outgoing dog that is playful and friendly. Despite its size, it is not afraid to join in with the action. It gets on well with both people and other dogs. It will bark vociferously when strangers approach.

Suitability as a pet A great first-time pet. It is as happy in an apartment as in a country house. It thrives on human companionship and responds well to training. Regular grooming is essential.

The toy group

Above A self-confident, active small dog which needs little exercise

Below A popular house dog, the Bichon Frisé responds well to human friendship making a loyal companion

Height 23–30 cm (9–11 in)
Weight 3–6 kg (7–12 lb)
Life span 14 years
Exercise *
Grooming ***
Town or Country T/C

Cavalier King Charles Spaniel

Bred originally to be both a companion and lap warmer, the Cavalier King Charles Spaniel is a happy-go-lucky, sociable dog that will adapt easily to its surroundings.

Origins By the seventeenth century selective spaniel breeding resulted in the toy breed, a favourite with King Charles II. Over the years its breed characteristics changed, until in 1926 a prize was offered for a dog that resembled those that appeared in Van Dyck's portrait of Charles II. Two years later it was awarded to 'Ann's son' and the Cavalier King Charles Spaniel was standardized.

Appearance A well-balanced, active dog that developed from the King Charles Spaniel but is slightly larger and has a longer muzzle. It has a long silky coat that can be in a variety of colours from Blenheim (chestnut and white), tricolour, ruby or black and tan. It has long, fringed ears.

Temperament As a miniature spaniel it has the typical characteristics of both a toy and gundog so enjoys exercise but is equally happy curled up by the fire. Affable, easily trained and playful.

The toy group

Suitability as a pet An excellent pet for the elderly as well as for a young family. It is good with children and relatively undemanding. Some grooming is essential.

Easy to groom, affable and in need of only moderate exercise, the Cavalier King Charles Spaniel can make an ideal pet

Height 31–3 cm (12–13 in)
Weight 5–8 kg (10–18 lb)
Life span 9–11 years
Exercise *
Grooming **
Town or Country T/C

Chihuahua (long coat and smooth coat)

The smallest of all breeds, the Chihuahua is a spirited little dog that can become attached to its owner to the point of jealousy and will fight back when provoked.

Origins Named after a Mexican state, it is thought that the chihuahua originated when the Aztecs crossed the heavier techichi dogs of the Toltec civilization with an Oriental hairless breed. The Aztecs considered Chihuahuas to be sacred. They were first exported to America in the 1850s and then around the world.

Appearance It can have either a smooth, short coat or a long soft one, both of which can be any colour. It has large upright ears and large eyes. Its tail is carried proudly aloft.

Temperament A lively, intelligent little dog with an engaging expression. Chihuahuas do not appreciate dogs of other breeds and are not afraid to stand up to them. They are curious and naughty and, despite their size, have often managed to manipulate their way to becoming master of the house.

The toy group

Suitability as a pet Ideal for an elderly person or a couple but not for a house of boisterous children, as they may injure it by mistake. It can bite when frightened so is happiest in a household where it is thoroughly pampered and in return will provide comfort and affection.

Right The Chihuahua has a feisty personality that is at least twice its size

Above An intrepid little guard dog, the Chihuahua will rush to defend its owner if it believes them to be threatened

Height 15–23 cm (6–9 in)
Weight 1–3 kg (2–6 lb)
Life span 13–14 years
Exercise *
Grooming *
Town or Country T/C

Chinese Crested Dog

Love it or loathe it, there's no doubt that the Chinese Crested Dog makes heads turn. This breed is not just appreciated for its novelty value, however – it also makes a faithful and amusing companion.

Origins Once the favoured pets of Chinese mandarins, these dogs are now extinct in China. Whether they originated there or in Africa is a matter of debate. They have existed in Central and South America for the last five centuries, presumably brought there by traders.

Appearance Puppies in the same litter can be born either with hair – 'powderpuffs' – or without – 'hairless'. They have long ears that are erect on the hairless and drooping on the powderpuff. Their fine hair can be a range of colours and on the hairless consists only of a crest on the head, a plume on the tail and a little hair on the feet. Both varieties are fine-boned and graceful.

Temperament Both powderpuff and hairless breeds are playful, affectionate and entertaining. Despite its thick skin, the hairless variety can feel the cold and may need special attention during the winter.

The toy group

Suitability as a pet They can be resistant to training but make good, intelligent pets, becoming particularly attached to their owner. The hairless variety is good for those who suffer from allergies.

The hairless Chinese Crested Dog has particularly thick skin for protection though it may need extra covering in winter

Height 23–33 cm (9–13 in)
Weight 2–5.5 kg (5–12 lb)
Life span 12–14 years
Exercise *
Grooming **
Town or Country T/C

Griffon Bruxellois

Renowned for its curious monkey face, the Griffon Bruxellois could be seen riding in the hansom cabs of late-nineteenth-century Brussels when it wasn't ratting in the stables.

Origins The breed was probably developed in Brussels, by crossing the Affenpinscher, King Charles Spaniel, Yorkshire Terrier and the pug. By 1890 it had become hugely popular, so much so that Anne, Queen of Belgium, took it up and it was exported to Britain.

Appearance A small dog, quite heavy for its size, the griffon bruxellois has a harsh, wiry coat, which is long- or smooth-haired and comes in red, black or black and tan. It has a pugnacious head with a prominent chin and, in the case of the long-haired variety, a distinguished walrus moustache and beard.

Temperament This is a friendly, outgoing creature that responds positively to obedience training and has a feisty and lively terrier temperament. It loves exercise but can be equally happy in more sedate surroundings.

Suitability as a pet The Griffon Bruxellois is equally at home as a member of a busy family or as a faithful companion to a single person.

Right The long-haired variety has a distinctive walrus moustache and beard

Above The smooth-coated version is just as lively and has the same bright questioning eyes that display the breed's intelligence

Height 18–20 cm (7–8 in)
Weight 2.5–5.5 kg (6–12 lb)
Life span 12–14 years
Exercise *
Grooming **
Town or Country T/C

King Charles Spaniel

A close relative of the Cavalier King Charles, this neat little dog is also known as the English Toy Spaniel. Popular with members of the court in Tudor England, it got its royal prefix when it became the favourite of King Charles II.

Origins Selective breeding of smaller spaniels led to the development of the English Toy Spaniel. The dogs of King Charles II were larger than those of today. It is thought that they may have been crossed with the Japanese Chin to produce the smaller dog with a squashed nose.

Appearance Often mistaken for the Cavalier King Charles Spaniel, the King Charles has a more turned-up nose squashed close to its skull. Its coat is long and wavy, usually black and tan, tricolour, Blenheim (white with chestnut red patches) or ruby (rich chestnut). A white blaze on the forehead with a red spot in the centre is a prized feature.

Temperament More reserved than the Cavalier King Charles, it is none the less an intelligent, good-natured dog which makes a delightful and devoted companion.

Suitability as a pet Its gentle, affectionate nature and its need for minimum exercise make it a superb pet, especially for the elderly.

This appealing small dog has a similar though quieter character to the Cavalier King Charles. Its snub nose is more pronounced

Height 25–7 cm (10–11 in)
Weight 4–6kg (8–14 lb)
Life span 11–12 years
Grooming **
Exercise *
Town/Country T/C

Papillon

Named after the French word for butterfly, because of its elegant ears and facial markings, this delicate little toy dog makes a highly intelligent, protective and affectionate companion.

Origins The Papillon was specifically bred from various toy spaniels to be a lapdog for the ladies of the sixteenth-century European courts. The Phalène (moth) is another version of the same dog – its ears are folded over like a moth at rest.

Appearance A fine-boned, active dog, it is particularly noted for its coat, head and tail. The glamorous coat is long and soft, always white, with markings of any colour except liver. The white stripe down the centre of its face represents the butterfly's body while its face and ears resemble the wings. The tail is extravagantly plumed and arches over the back.

Temperament Not surprisingly, both the Papillon and the Phalène have spaniel personalities: cheerful, alert and amenable. They are very intelligent, easily trained and will even excel in obedience competitions.

The toy group

Suitability as a pet Not a pet for a family with small children. They are extremely affectionate and can be fiercely protective. It is surprisingly robust for its size but will need daily grooming to keep up appearances.

The Papillon is an enchanting small dog whose long, silky coat hides a bright, obedient personality

Height 20–8 cm (8–11 in)
Weight 4–4.5 kg (9–10 lb)
Life span 13–15 years
Exercise *
Grooming * * *
Town or Country T/C

Pekingese

According to Chinese legend, the Pekingese is the result of the union of a monkey and a lion, hence both its grace and nobility. It has become the last word in lapdogs, content to rest companionably on a sofa or knee.

Origins Its origins are unclear but Pekingese have certainly led a privileged life in the Chinese imperial courts. They were one of the 'sleeve dogs' carried in the capacious sleeves of royal garments. In 1860, five were brought back by British troops, who presented one to Queen Victoria, ensuring their immediate popularity.

Appearance It has a wide head and a short muzzle, which may exacerbate breathing problems. Its abundant coat may be of any colour but albino or liver.

Temperament The Pekingese has a regal nature and is noted for its bad temper. However, this may be due more to the owner than to the dog itself.

Suitability as a pet It is not always easy to train or house-train. It is a devoted one-person pet for someone prepared to take special care with the delicate grooming it requires. Not suitable for a family with young children.

The toy group

Above As this Pekingese puppy grows, its coat will become longer and thicker until its body shape is effectively concealed

Above Pekingese have pretty heads with large soulful eyes that appeal to the many owners who appreciate its lapdog qualities

Height 15–23 cm (6–9 in)
Weight 3–6 kg (7–12 lb)
Life span 12–13 years
Exercise *
Grooming * * *
Town or Country T

Pomeranian

This tiny puffball of a dog may enjoy being spoilt but it also has the attractive character of a much larger dog – active, outgoing and fun.

Origins The Pomeranian is the smallest of the spitz breeds. It is believed to have originated in Pomerania, Germany, before being brought to Britain in the eighteenth century where, over the subsequent decades, it was bred to be even smaller. This is another dog popularized by Queen Victoria, who welcomed it into her kennels.

Appearance Its bright little face is surrounded by a ruff which is typical of the Arctic spitzes. Its slight body is covered with a thick undercoat and a long straight topcoat, which can be black, grey, blue, brown, rust or cream-white and sable. Its tail curls like a plume over its back.

Temperament This is a feisty bundle of fun that loves to show off. It has an extremely friendly and inquisitive nature and makes a great watchdog, in spite of its small size.

The toy group

Suitability as a pet Ideal for someone with limited space. Although Pomeranians love children they are not robust enough to put up with too much rough and tumble. They are intelligent and can be easily trained. It's essential to curb their barking at an early age if you want to live in peace. Regular grooming is paramount.

This captivating fluff ball of a dog is confident and smart. It makes a good pet but needs a lot of attention when it comes to grooming

Height 22–8 cm (8.5–11 in)
Weight 2–3 kg (4–5.5 lb)
Life span 15 years
Exercise *
Grooming * * *
Town or Country T

Pug

The Pug is a miniaturized form of the Tibetan mastiffs originally kept by Buddhists before being brought to the West. Its gentle nature makes it a splendid pint-size companion.

Origins Bred as a lapdog in the Orient, the breed is thought to have been transported to Holland by the Dutch East India Company in the 1500s. William III introduced it to England when he assumed the throne in 1688. It soon became the rage and later became another favourite of Queen Victoria.

Appearance A sturdy, compact little dog whose tightly curled tail almost matches the neatness of its stubby expressive face. Its short, sleek coat comes in black, silver, fawn or apricot. Despite a jaunty, slightly rolling gait, the Pug can move quickly and enjoys playing.

Temperament It has a stable, good-natured and extrovert personality and will also make a good watchdog. The story goes that a Pug warned William III of the approach of the Spanish, thus enabling him to escape. The breed has been celebrated ever after.

Suitability as a pet Its affectionate nature means it is great with children or elderly people. Pugs can be wilful and testing to train but are low-maintenance, low-activity dogs that need little grooming.

The Pug is a picture of strength. It has a muscular build with sturdy straight legs and a distinctive curled tail. Its expressive wrinkled brow makes it most appealing

Height 25–8 cm (10–11 in)
Weight 6–8 kg (14–18 lb)
Life span 13–14 years
Exercise *
Grooming *
Town or Country T/C

Yorkshire Terrier

This lively, indomitable breed needs little exercise but adores the opportunity to play. However spirited it may be, it can always be relied on both for its loyalty and its lively companionship.

Origins The earliest Yorkshire Terriers were bred by miners in the north of England to catch rats and other vermin. The miners crossed the Clydesdale terrier with the English Black-and-tans, Skye and Maltese terriers. Today the Yorkshire Terrier is only bred for show and for companionship.

Appearance A small, glamorous dog that gives off an unmistakable sense of its own importance. It is noted for its fine long coat that has straight, steel-blue hair on the body and tan hair everywhere else. The body is compact and tidy. It has a small head with bright, intelligent eyes and prick ears. The tail is most often docked.

Temperament It may be tiny but this breed nevertheless retains its terrier instincts. It is spirited but with an even disposition.

The toy group

Suitability as a pet Hugely popular in the city, where there is little space. It may show aggression to other dogs but being so small it can be picked up before any trouble starts. Extremely territorial, its barking can be a problem with the neighbours. Regular grooming is a must.

Sparkling eyes and a lively disposition make the Yorkshire Terrier one of the most popular of the toy breeds

Height 22.5–3.5 cm (9 in)
Weight 2.5–3.5 kg (5–7 lb)
Life span 14 years
Exercise *
Grooming **
Town or Country T/C

The utility (non-sporting) group

This is a group of breeds that was introduced in 1967, having previously been known as the 'non-sporting group', as it still is in America and Australia. It comprises miscellaneous breeds from all over the world that do not readily fit into the other groups. Another term used for this group is the 'companion group', although some are naturally more friendly than others. Some of them, such as

Above left The Dalmatian's stamina and affinity with horses made it an elegant and tireless carriage dog. *Above right* The spitz breeds developed in the Arctic and were used primarily for hunting, guarding and pulling sledges.

the Dalmatian and the Bulldog, find their place in this group because the jobs they were bred to do no longer exist. Others, such as the Shar-pei or Lhasa Apso, are here because of their unusual appearance. These are also some of the oldest documented breeds in the world.

All in all they are a very mixed bunch indeed. There are a number of spitz-type breeds, such as the Chow-chow, Japanese Spitz, Keeshond and Schipperke. These all have the recognizable features of the perky ears, straight hind legs, luxuriant neck ruff and tightly curled tail. Dogs that were originally used for sporting purposes that no longer exist include the British and French Bulldogs, which were used for bull baiting, and the poodle, which, with its strong sense of smell, was used to retrieve waterfowl even by night. Feisty terrier qualities are found in the Dalmatian and Schnauzer. These two breeds ran beside carriages to defend travellers and were also used as ratters and vermin-hunters. Other dogs in the group, such as the exotic Shih-tzu, were bred solely as companions.

Bulldog

The Bulldog has come to epitomize grit and determination. Yet its solid, belligerent appearance masks a surprisingly sweet temper.

Origins The breed was most popular when animal baiting was at its height. Used to fight bulls, bears and badgers, the Bulldog was developed so that it could grab a bull by the nose and hang on until the bull collapsed. Bull baiting was banned across the world in 1835 but the bulldog went on to become a gentle-natured show dog and companion.

Appearance Once seen never forgotten. The Bulldog is well built with its legs squarely set at each corner of its body, giving it a distinct waddle. Its squashy face was designed for bullfighting but this does also mean it can get out of breath when over-exercised. Its coat is short and comes in a number of different colours.

Temperament Despite appearances, this is not an aggressive dog. Instead, it is calm, kind and engaging. It makes a very good watchdog, largely because of its looks rather than its bark, which is somewhat infrequent.

Suitability as a pet It can stick in its heels when it comes to training so may need gentle coercion. It generally loves children and succeeds in getting on with other dogs by ignoring them.

Right Its stance is full square and uncompromising but don't be deceived. This is a gentle and companionable dog

Above The memorable face of the Bulldog has earned it the nickname of 'Old Sourmug'

Height 31–6 cm (12–14 in)
Weight 23–5 kg (50–5 lb)
Life span 7–10 years
Grooming *
Exercise *
Town or Country T/C

Chow-chow

Legend has it that the Chow-chow got its blue-black tongue by lapping up the drops of paint that fell when God was painting the sky blue.

Origins The Mongolians used the Chow-chow for its hunting and guarding qualities as well as for its meat and fur. It is thought to have descended from the spitz breeds that were brought to Britain in the late eighteenth century by sailors returning from the East.

Appearance Square-bodied with a thick coat in cream, fawn, red, blue or black. It has a tightly curled tail and small prick ears. Its slightly stiff gait makes movement slow. The inside of its mouth and its tongue are black.

Temperament An intelligent dog with a mind of its own. It is not the cuddly bundle of fun it may appear. It is wary of strangers though loyal to its owner.

Suitability as a pet The Chow-chow is not a family pet. It is easily house-trained but often stubborn in learning the art of obedience. It makes a quiet, rather aloof pet that will fiercely defend its owner and territory. It doesn't befriend other dogs easily.

The utility group

Loyal to its owner, the Chow-chow is less friendly to strangers and is occasionally considered to be rather bad-tempered and obstinate

Height 46–56 cm (18–22 in)
Weight 20–32 kg (45–70 lb)
Life span 11–12 years
Grooming * *
Exercise * *
Town or Country T/C

Dalmatian

No other dog has such a distinctively marked coat. The Dalmatian has performed a number of jobs over the years and today makes a lively and attractive companion that needs plenty of exercise.

Origins There is evidence that Dalmatians have been around for thousands of years. More recently they have been used as carriage dogs, running close to the wheels. The breed was also used in American fire departments in the nineteenth century to control the horses that pulled the fire appliances.

Appearance A lean, muscular dog that can run to fat if not sufficiently exercised. The coat is white when the pups are born and the brown or black spots develop over the first few weeks.

Temperament Can vary across the breed though generally intelligent, energetic and friendly.

Suitability as a pet This is a dog that loves people. Easy to groom and train but needing regular exercise to prevent it from becoming neurotic or destructive. A great addition to any family willing to pay it enough attention.

Its unique spotty coat has long made the Dalmatian a popular pet. However, because of its tendency to fat, it needs lots of exercise

Height 50–61 cm (20–4 in)
Weight 23–5 kg (50–5 lb)
Life span 12 years
Grooming *
Exercise * *
Town or Country T/C

Keeshond

Also known as the 'smiling Dutchman', this breed is still a favourite in its native Holland. Its magnificent appearance and affectionate nature make it a dog to be proud of.

Origins The Keeshond was first used as a watchdog on the Dutch barges and was named after Cornelius 'Kees' de Gyzelaar, the leader of the Dutch Patriot Revolt which took place in the eighteenth century. As a result of this it became the symbol of the Patriot Party but soon fell into decline when the party fell from power. A century later, it was introduced to Britain and then America, where it is one of the most popular of the spitz breeds.

Appearance A solid, muscular dog, the keeshond has an impressive silver-grey coat with a ruff at the neck and a tightly curled tail. It has small prick ears, a shortish muzzle and an endearing smile.

Temperament This is an outgoing, amiable dog that needs firm handling if it is not to to be troublesome to its owner.

The utility group

Suitability as a pet If trained properly, this spitz will become an affectionate and devoted pet. It loves being part of family activities and will also make a good watchdog. It sheds its coat intensely twice a year and needs regular grooming and exercise.

The Keeshond has all the hallmarks of the spitz breeds: pricked ears, solid body and a curled tail

Height 43–8 cm (17–19 in)
Weight 25–30 kg (55–66 lb)
Life span 12–14 years
Exercise * *
Grooming * *
Town or Country T/C

Lhasa Apso

These exotic, glamorous-looking dogs are in fact tough little animals, bred to be indoor watchdogs in the monasteries of Tibet. Their name derives from Lhasa, the capital of Tibet, and 'apso', which means goat-like, sentinel or long-haired dog.

Origins The breed was developed in Tibet, where it made an effective temple guard dog. It was deemed a holy creature and a gift of one was thought to be a sign of good fortune. It was brought to Britain in 1901.

Appearance Its long, tough coat, which provided protection against the severe climate of Tibet, can be of any colour or a mix of colours. Its head is small with dark eyes, while its tail is screwed over its back.

Temperament These bright dogs have an acute sense of hearing, which explains why they are such good guard dogs. They like human company but are very much a one-person dog and can be haughty with strangers.

Suitability as a pet An affectionate, loyal lapdog that will reward an owner who puts in the effort to train and groom it. Absolutely not for children.

The utility group

Above Despite its long coat, the Lhasa Apso can walk for miles without complaint

Above Originally indoor guard dogs, the Lhasa Apso has become a self-confident, appreciative pet

Height 25–8 cm (10–11 in)
Weight 6–7 kg (13–15 lb)
Life span 12–14 years
Grooming * * *
Exercise *
Town or Country T

Poodle

A versatile, intelligent and good-natured dog, the Poodle originated in Germany as a water dog, where it retrieved the fallen birds for the hunters.

Origins Its name derives from the German 'pudeln' (to splash in water). The popularity of the Standard Poodle led to the miniature and toy varieties being developed. It has been a retriever, a circus performer and a favourite with the French royal household.

Appearance A well-proportioned, proud-looking animal with a distinctive curly coat and a springy gait. The coat comes in black, white, chocolate, apricot, silver and blue, and does not shed. Often the most distinctive thing about the Poodle is its clip. There are a number of different clips, the most common being the puppy clip and sporting clip. Pompoms decorate the end of the tail.

Temperament Renowned as one of the most intelligent dogs of all, the Poodle is easily trained. Its character varies with its size – the standard is calm, independent, friendly and learns fast while the smaller sizes can be more demanding and more active.

The utility group

Suitability as a pet Makes an excellent family dog as it enjoys playing with children, joining in activities and guarding the house. Grooming can be time-consuming, the choice of clips being best done by a professional.

The Poodle is regarded as one of the most intelligent dogs. They respond well to training and make great pets

(Standard Poodle)
Height 37.5–8.5 cm (15 in)
Weight 20.5–32 kg (45–70 lb)
Life span 12–13 years
Grooming * * *
Exercise * *
Town or Country T/C

Schipperke

This hardy dog is also known as the 'little captain', because of its original role as a guard dog and ratter on Belgian barges. It was used on land to hunt small vermin.

Origins Of classic spitz appearance, the Schipperke's origins are unclear. It is thought that it may have begun life as one of the following: a miniature of the black Belgian sheepdog; a descendant of the spitz breeds; or a cross between a German Pomeranian and a terrier.

Appearance It has a compact body with a deep chest. It has a short neck, prick ears and a tail that if not docked will curl spitz-like on its back. Its thick, harsh coat is usually black, long on the body with a slight ruff, and smooth on the head.

Temperament An active, intelligent and curious dog, the schipperke has a will of its own. It does, however, respond well to kindness and can be easily trained.

Suitability as a pet This breed can be domineering if not trained early. It will be devoted to a family, enjoying moderate exercise without being too demanding. Its sharp hearing makes it an excellent watchdog.

The utility group

The Schipperke loves exercise, has an easy-going temperament and makes an excellent guard dog

Height 22–33 cm (9–13 in)
Weight 3–8 kg (7–18 lb)
Exercise * *
Grooming *
Town or Country T/C

Schnauzer

The Schnauzer comes in three sizes: giant, standard and miniature. All of them are jaunty, affectionate dogs that are renowned for their fidelity and bravery.

Origins A German breed whose portrait appeared in paintings of the fifteenth and sixteenth centuries. Probably a cross between the German Poodle and a spitz, the Schnauzer has always been a working dog and has been used as a rat catcher, a herder, a guard dog and as a Red Cross aide and dispatch carrier during the Second World War. The giant and miniature varieties evolved from the standard.

Appearance A compact dog with a short wiry coat that comes in black or what is known as 'pepper and salt'. It has thick, 'Colonel Blimpish' eyebrows and a distinctive beard.

Temperament 'The big dog in a small body' describes the standard Schnauzer. It is a gentle, friendly dog which has bags of character. Its highly developed senses have also earned it the description 'the dog with the human brain'.

The utility group

Suitability as a pet A great all-rounder. Larger breeds need training to curb their sometimes headstrong nature. The Giant Schnauzer makes a lively, trustworthy guard dog. Recommended for people allergic to other breeds.

Right The standard Schnauzer is a compact energetic dog which can be an asset to active families

Above The Schnauzers are distinguished by their bushy eyebrows and thick beards

(standard schnauzer)
Height 45–50 cm (18–20 in)
Weight 14.5–15.5 kg (32–4 lb)
Life span 12–14 years
Grooming *
Exercise * *
Town or Country T/C

Shar-pei

The Shar-pei's bristly, wrinkled skin has acted as protection from human or animal attackers and won it favour as a fighting dog in ancient China. All but extinct by the 1950s, the breed has been revived more recently by Hong Kong breeders.

Origins It was used as a fighting dog until traders brought in larger mastiff types from the West, when it became a domestic pet that guarded the home. In communist China dogs were considered a luxury and heavily taxed so the breed began to die out.

Appearance With its stocky stance, extraordinary hippopotamus-like head and great folds of skin, the shar-pei is an unmistakable creature. Its coat comes in three lengths, horse, brush or bear, and in red, fawn, cream, apricot or black.

Temperament Not always the most perfectly behaved dog, it tends to be independent or aloof with strangers yet devoted to its owner. Regarded as an excellent watchdog, though not aggressive to other people or other dogs.

Suitability as a pet This breed is more of a one-man dog than a family pet. It needs to be properly socialized as a puppy and trained carefully so that any aggressive streak is controlled. Once its place in the pecking order has been established, it will be a loyal friend.

The extraordinary looking Shar-Pei is a strongly built dog with a large head, fleshy muzzle and somewhat bemused expression

Height 46–51 cm (18–20 in)
Weight 16–20 kg (25–45 lb)
Life span 11–12 years
Grooming * *
Exercise * *
Town or Country T/C

Shih-tzu

A breed with its roots deep in history, the Shih-tzu is perfect for someone with the time and patience to spend tirelessly grooming a loving and regal lapdog.

Origins One of the Tibetan 'lion dogs', which also include the Lhasa Apso and the Tibetan Spaniel. In the mid-nineteenth century Shih-tzus were presented to the Manchu emperors of Peking, where they became court favourites. They were brought to England in 1930 by Lady Brownrigg and made their way to America with the GIs during the Second World War.

Appearance The long, dense coat comes in many colours. The hair tends to grow upwards on the nose and is gathered into a ponytail on the top of the head, revealing button-black eyes and a nose that sports a distinguished moustache.

Temperament A feisty little dog that can be both proud and stubborn. It demands the treatment of a king and usually gets it. Persistence will pay off in training this intelligent dog to become a reliable companion and watchdog.

Suitability as a pet The Shih-tzu will fit into a family though may feel jealous of the attention given to babies and toddlers. Its bouncy, robust nature will endear it to everyone, not least the person who does the grooming.

A small dog that is absolutely confident of its own superiority. An outgoing nature makes it an enjoyable pet, though the grooming duties are considerable

Height 25–7 cm (10–11 in)
Weight 5–7 kg (10–16 lb)
Life span 12–14 years
Grooming * * *
Exercise *
Town or Country T

Index of dog breeds